T0309502

Wine and Space

Heinz-Gert Woschek   Denis Duhme   Katrin Friederichs

W I N E
+
S P A C E

Architectural design for vinotheques, wine bars and shops

Edition **DETAIL**

Authors: Heinz-Gert Woschek (editor), Denis Duhme,
Katrin Friederichs

Editors: Cosima Frohnmaier, Cornelia Hellstern
(project manager), Florian Köhler, Kai Meyer

Editorial services: Theresa Steinel,
Dr. Ilka Backmeister-Collacott

Translations and copy-editing: Christine Madden, Munich;
Kathrin Enke, Ludwigsburg; Elizabeth Kay-Müller, Geretsried

Illustrations: Simon Kramer, Ralph Donhauser

Graphic design: HiltbrunnerDesign, Munich

Production and layout: Roswitha Siegler

Reproduction: ludwig:media, Zell am See

Printing and binding: Kösel GmbH & Co. KG,
Altusried-Krugzell

© 2015, first edition
DETAIL – Institut für internationale Architektur-
Dokumentation GmbH & Co. KG, München
www.detail.de

ISBN 978-3-95553-241-3 (Print)
ISBN 978-3-95553-242-0 (E-Book)
ISBN 978-3-95553-243-7 (Bundle)

This work is subject to copyright. All rights reserved, whether
the whole or part of the material is concerned, specifically
the rights of translation, reprinting, recitation, reuse of illustrations and tables, broadcasting, reproduction on microfilm
or in other ways, and storage in data processing systems.
Reproduction of any part of this work in individual cases, too,
is only permitted within the limits of the provisions of the
valid edition of the copyright law. A charge will be levied.
Infringements will be subject to the penalty clauses of the
copyright law.

Bibliographical information published by the German
National Library. The German National Library lists this
publication in the Deutsche Nationalbibliografie; d
etailed bibliographical data are available on the Internet at
http://dnb.d-nb.de.

MIX
Papier aus verantwor-
tungsvollen Quellen
FSC® C013736

Contents

Monvínic wine bar and restaurant in Barcelona (Spain). Their cellar contains about 3,000 different wines from all over the world.

Foreword

Enjoying wine – the cult

Since antiquity, wine has assumed a unique place in the lives of people in civilised societies. It is exceptional not only in its sheer variety but also in the sense of its value, which far exceeds its presence as a commodity. No other agricultural product nor any luxury good, nor stimulant has ever been able to achieve equal significance. The exceptional effects wine is known to elicit, however, only relate to its immediate sensory and intoxicating aspects. Wine is sometimes described as something beyond this, a "divine" beverage equated to sacred mystery.

But the once transcendent correlation of wine to the mythical and supernatural has long become a relic of the past. Instead of Dionysius, Bacchus or mediaeval wine saints, contact with and exposure to wine reveal other contents. The spectrum of modern "wine culture" ranges from classical forms of presentation in the visual arts and music and successful designs for displaying and presenting wine as a product to the various activities in which its appearance in folklore or festivities is celebrated. The "mystery of wine" has therefore been succeeded by the "fascination of wine".

Changes such as these were only possible when wine became more accessible as a consumer product. The qualities of wine today, and the way it is made, only share a few rudimentary aspects with the product bearing the same name in earlier centuries. Crucial characteristics of the product – such as a particular amount of healthfulness, reliable standards of quality and dependable designation of origin and manner of presentation – have in recent years stimulated the increasing popularity of wine consumption. Worldwide distribution and availability as well as a broad pricing structure have opened almost every trading channel and market segment for this "vine juice" – from folkloristic table wine to the elite, luxury beverage. Independent of quantitative growth, there have been meaningful changes in the quality of the product that, as a consequence of the significant improvements in production methods, has increased globally. With regard to wine production, these are in particular the focus on proven and internationally preferred grape varieties, rationalised processing and harvesting methods. This basis has been complemented in viniculture by the latest technology – often combined with traditional winemaking techniques, for example the use of oak barrels.

A brief profile of contemporary winemaking such as this, however, cannot hope to cover every oenological practice. In fact, numerous variations lead to the actual individual character of wine as a product. The differences result from the contrast between the inexpensive, industrially produced product to artisan wine as an example of authentic wine production. In actual fact, specific environmental factors – particularly climate, region and soil (which is described by the professional term "terroir") – contribute to the distinctive originality of a given wine. And it is precisely the recognition of these characteristics and their influence on the image of a specific wine that makes working with wine as a cultural product more and more of an inducement and pleasure. In this way, one also experiences "culture" in a variety of ways – both in its most basic form as "agri-culture", and – particularly – in its noble manifestation, as an sensory experience, as a stimulant and, last but not least, as a catalyst for conviviality and communication.

In this way, the cult of wine has now come to extend into the most diverse areas of life. As a companion to contemporary gastronomy, it plays as indispensable a role as it does for wine tourism, as centrepiece of cultural wine events or as collector's item, investment and status symbol. Last but not least, being a wine connoisseur enhances personal prestige, so that acquiring knowledge about wine has become a popular hobby.

Suppliers are an important element in this chain, ranging from producing to enjoying wine. Whatever link one occupies in the chain – consultant, expert, salesperson, sommelier or restaurateur – the same function is always involved: awakening interest, taste and enthusiasm in potential customers and guests with eloquence, knowledge and integrity. The collected examples from the diverse display and marketing sectors in this book show that environment, ambience and interior, architecture and design and a specially designated space to experience wine play an integral role for each of these venues in enabling this kind of exchange.

In our first volume, *Wine and Architecture,* we touched only marginally on the sales-orientated presentation of wine in keeping with the specific theme of the book. But because of the importance of marketing and display for successful sales in wine production, the wine market and the gastronomic sector, this volume will concentrate on the presentation of exemplary projects that are each typical of the large spectrum of wine marketing in Europe. Together, they not only convey interesting inspirations for architectural and design solutions but also reflect on the captivating vista of contemporary wine culture.

Heinz-Gert Woschek
June 2014

Introduction

Enjoying wine – a short history

Wine culture and quality of life

Wine production is considered to be a pillar of western wine culture. But people frequently overlook the fact that, without wine marketing and venues, it would neither have spread internationally nor achieved its traditional importance. This is because the sale and serving of wine have as long a tradition as its cultivation and production.

The Romans brought the "business model" of serving wine, which they adopted from the Greeks, to a high point. To store the wine at home, they used the *cella vinaria* – a wine vault or cellar. The general public, who didn't have this option at their disposal, kept their wine purchases in a *horreum* – an often multi-storey, extensive public storage and emporium. Along with the *tabernae* (restaurants) and *tabernae vinaria* (wine taverns), it was a central marketplace, but also a shopping and communication centre.

These venues represented a social function for the quality of life of free citizens of imperial Rome. In contrast to the *cauponae,* the food shops, the *tabernae* principally supported the pleasure of drinking; wine was served here mixed with water and spices, honey or other ingredients. Additionally, a generally small selection of food items would be served. Some establishments offered the possibility of overnight lodging in an adjacent room – a feature that later developed into the *hospitium* (hotel or guest house). The specific form of external marketing with which these venues still attract attention today was already in practice 2000 years ago: signs with familiar animal names ("The Swan", "The Eagle", "The Elephant") were then already in use.

A *taberna* was often a long, narrow space with a broad entrance, wooden ceiling and one window. At the centre there would be an L or U-shaped bar with *dolia* (fat, barrel-like earthenware pots, their interior lined with tar) along the sides, which were filled with wine or other products. The guest area would also feature shelving and a fireplace. As a colourful combination of wine tavern, pub and restaurant, the Roman *tabernae* represent the first manifestation of restaurant. This only

Far left: Termopolio della via Diana in the ancient Roman harbour city Ostia Antica (Italy). Equipped with a counter, racks and benches, this tavern and wine bar from the 3rd century BCE gives a taste of Roman wine gastronomy. Various entrances fitted with stoneware vessels for wine and oil *(dolia)* lead to the dining room and the kitchen.

Left: Weingut (wine estate) Poss in Windesheim/Nahe (Germany). The original cellar walls of a Roman *villa rustica* dating from the 1st to 4th century CE, which contained wine amphoras, were discovered during the new construction of the wine shop on the premises and integrated into the tasting area – accessible through the shop.

Right: Bremer Ratskeller (Bremen town hall cellar) (Germany). The Ratskeller is one of Germany's oldest taverns and, as part of the town hall, a UNESCO world cultural heritage site. Its central attraction is the "Great Hall" – 300 m² supported by 20 stone columns – in which wine has been served sine 1405. The hall has three naves and contains four lavishly decorated barrels from the 18th century. (Image ca. 1900)

changed its structure when modes of trade that were once separate and distinct began to be intensively combined.

What can be seen as the official beginning of the wine bar was the granting of wine marketing licences by the Carolingian empire for the establishment of seasonal wine taverns, known for example as *"Straußwirtschaften"* or *"Kranzwirtschaften"*. In German-speaking wine-producing countries, these are still known as *Besenwirtschaften* or *Heckenwirtschaften.* They encompass the winemaker's temporary serving and sale of his own wines along with with rustic specialities from the region. These establishments, with their homely local colour, developed into the winemaker's tasting rooms and, subsequently, the shop and display area.

In contrast to this rustic, rather easy-going ambience, wine gastronomy and marketing in the contemporary urban environment has taken off. The expansion of transport routes and the historic significance of important cities on these routes were influenced by the roaring trade in wines since the Middle Ages. Wine sellers and brokers helped transform these relevant market and fair locations into well-known centres for wine transactions and sales. The impressive wine cellars in the basement vaults of town halls, particularly in Hanseatic League cities, attest to prosperity and economic significance. Initially used as strictly guarded and – thanks to walls that were metres thick – well-tempered urban wine warehouses, these grand vaulted cellars soon developed into popular venues for the urban population to meet and drink wine.

In the 18th and in particular the 19th century, a wave of new commercial enterprises started up that initially offered a broad spectrum of products (particularly colonial wares), but which later came to concentrate on wines and spirits. Many sellers had their transformation from grocery to specialised shop to thank for their reputation as knowledgeable, reliable wine merchants – their position in society also depended on the trust prominent customers had in them. One example of this would be the Ramann Brothers wine merchants in Erfurt, whose clientele included, among others, many famous classical poets in the circle of the renowned German writers Johann Wolfgang von Goethe and Friedrich Schiller.

Until late in the 18th century, sales of wine were conducted exclusively with "casks": wooden barrels of diverse sizes. Accordingly, wine warehouses and sales establishments hardly looked any different from cellars and wine businesses. At their centre would be rooms for storing barrels of various sizes – particularly the "Ohm" (app 150 litres), the "Viertelstück" (app 300 litres) or the "Doppelstück" (app 600 litres) – measures once widely used in central Europe. Later, importers and wholesalers also carried out their own bottle filling. Actual commercial business took place in the "comptoir". Next to the office there would be rooms for wine tasting, which would highlight the time-honoured atmosphere of traditional wine shops.

Mechanical production of standardised wine bottle shapes, the use of corks as bottle stoppers and the declaration of contents on the accompanying labels ushered in an entirely new era of wine marketing. The shops, *"en gros und en detail mit Bouteillen"* (wholesale and retail with bottles), replaced traditional marketing with "open wares" (in barrels). The storage rooms for wooden barrels and the collection of demijohns got increasingly smaller with the establishment of bottle warehouses, which were influenced by new kinds of packaging, such as wooden crates for six or 12 bottles.

Above all, enormous logistic improvements made it possible to buy wine in resealable bottles that could be stored for longer periods of time. Thanks to this, wine became part of a sophisticated and representative lifestyle. Although the elements of wine display people used previously to make an impression were limited to exclusive accessories such as glasses and carafes, the ritual of wine tastings were developed within the circle of knowledgeable wine drinkers and collectors. Wine cellars in private homes, stocked with fine wines, became a status symbol. In *Das Weinbuch,* author Dr Wilhelm Hamm complained in 1865 that "in modern houses" people would find a good wine cellar much more seldom than in older buildings. "It may be partly because the expansion of wine marketing at present makes the private collection of wine unnecessary, which used to be considered a vital feature of a well equipped household."

The opportunity to raise the presentation of wine to

Far left: Auerbachs Keller in Leipzig (Germany). Founded in 1525, it is considered one of the most well-known wine restaurants. Its artistically designed wine room and Großer Keller (grand cellar) are unique. German author Goethe was a frequent guest and immortalised the Großer Keller in his tragic play *Faust*.

Centre left: Riesling Weingut (wine estate) Robert Weil in Kiedrich / Rheingau (Germany). The garden hall in the estate house dating from the 19th century is a typical example of salon culture; tastings of wine from the estate used to take place there.

Near left: "Haus Samson" in Leer (Germany). The house was building in 1570 and has been the home of the Wein Wolff shop since 1800. The historic interior has been maintained to this day.

Right: Originally from Mainz, Lorenz Adlon was initially a wine merchant before he opened his famous luxury hotel in Berlin in 1907. The distinctive interior of the building also includes the legendary climate-controlled wine cellar, in which famous estate wines were stored by the barrel and filled into bottles. When Russian soldiers plundered the gigantic store of wine in 1945, it started the fire that destroyed the hotel. This image from 1913 shows a waiter at the champagne refrigerator in the large kitchen.

Below: A "princely" wine tasting in Schloss Johannisberg (Germany). The building was completed in 1721. Surrounded by *halbstück* barrels and the mouldy walls in the barrel-vaulted, 260 m-long cellar, nobles and prominent wine estate owners gathered together on 1 November 1897 for a tasting. Standing (from left): J. J. von Zimmermann, Prinz von Metternich's comptroller; I. Heinisch, Metternich's demesne inspector; H. Allinger, Metternich's cellar master. Sitting (from left): Dr Clemens Wenzel von Metternich-Winneburg; C. Nobile dei Baroni Aliotti; Prince Franz von und zu Liechtenstein; A. Czéh, royal Prussian demesne councillor; Rudolf Goethe, royal Prussian state economic councillor; H. W. Dahlen, secretary-general of the German Wine-Growing Association; A. Dorn, administrator to his royal majesty Prince Albert of Prussia; Karl Prileszki von Prilesz, imperial director of the exchequer, Vienna.

particular glory by assembling an imposing collection of bottles from many famous wine regions, areas and producers was one that many restaurant and hotel owners enthusiastically grasped. Artistically decorated, wrought-iron wine racks, as well as extensive wine menus, became stylish treasure troves for guests, frequently augmented by a "wine treasury" featuring exquisite grape varieties. When Lorenz Adlon – who already operated a respected wine shop in Berlin – opened his famous hotel in 1907, it boasted, among many other attractions, a grand wine cellar with more than 100,000 bottles – which hardly any other grand hotel of that time could match.

In subsequent years, profound political, economic, social and cultural events led to radical changes in marketing and the restaurant industry. Companies that had up to then dominated the market with their domestic and imported acquisitions had to face up to competition from a diverse array of warehouse and specialised shops that also dealt in wine. Estates and vintners' associations conducted their own wine sales to brokers, restaurateurs and consumers – just like wine estates had previously opened branches in large cities hundreds of years before. Wine makers who sold their own products used alternative methods. They opened cellars, warehouses for bottled wine and their "salons" to

visits from customers and created an appropriate atmosphere for wine tastings.

With the beginnings of "wine tourism" in European wine regions, the success story of the *vinotheque,* or specialised wine boutique, began – whether as a community establishment on a local or regional level, or as a modern element of a wine estate's marketing activity.

Just as the spread and specialisation of wines for sale replaced the monopoly of classical wine and spirit shops in the second half of the previous century, the hotel and restaurant industry also experienced its own structural revolution. Changing consumption and consumer behaviours prompted the establishment of innovative new wine warehouses, wine depots and wine shops, which offered an international assortment of wine in stylish, modern and unconventional surroundings. At the same time, wine boutiques, wine bars and bodegas sprang up among the traditional wine taverns and classic wine restaurants to became special meeting places or favoured venues for purchasing wine. This heterogeneity gives the best insight into the way the wine's image transformed from traditional cultural heritage to youthful lifestyle product. And it seems as though this transformation process is in no way completed. The continuing development of our relationship with wine looks certain to remain intriguing in the future.

Wine as a product

Analytical composition of wine

In chemical terms, wine is grape juice processed and refined through fermentation. This simple description, however, says little about the complex composition of the product. Wine's hundreds of components, and the subsequently innumerable characteristics that they elicit, influence our senses and have a complex effect on body and soul.

Analytically speaking, water is by content the greatest leading component (about 700–900 mg/litre). Nevertheless, wine receives its typical character from an array of solid and liquid substances, acids, dissolved gases, mineral salts and, last but not least, numerous trace elements. The respective amounts of these elements derive from a multitude of natural factors, such as the variety, cultivation and ripeness of the processed grapes as well as geological influences (terroir, location) and climactic conditions. Wine processing plays a large role in the individual composition of a wine's makeup – starting with the harvest to the kind and length of fermentation, the handling of the young wine, maturation, storage and ultimately bottling and bottle storage.

During the fermentation of the must, yeasts transform the fructose and glucose in the grapes into alcohol (ethanol) and carbon dioxide. By controlling fermentation, this process can be influenced by temperature, yeast variety and special elements (such as sulphur dioxide). The results are accordingly diverse: the alcohol content of fermented wine ranges from about 7 to 16 per cent.

Aroma and taste are heavily influenced by the amount of non-volatile compounds – solid substances – in the wine. Non-volatile compounds can include carbohydrates, glycerol, non-volatile acids, nitrogen compounds, tannins, pigments, higher alcohols and minerals. Including sugar content, the amount of a wine's non-volatile compounds may vary between 16 and 30 g per litre. Red wines generally contain more non-volatile compounds than white wines because of their higher phenol (tannin) content. According to traditional notions, red wine should contain more than double the amount of non-volatile compounds than alcohol; for white wines, more than one and a half times as much. Lower alcohol content, however, doesn't necessarily mean that the wine has fewer non-volatile compounds – as the lower percentage of alcohol in white wines from the Mosel and Rhine can attest.

Apart from residual sugar (the content of which usually lies below 2 g per litre in fully fermented wine), the taste spectrum of wine is primarily determined by its organic acid content (acidity). Analytically speaking, this is made up of volatile and non-volatile acids (total acidity). The EU stipulates a minimum of 4.5 g per litre total acidity, with an upper limit of 8 g per litre for very acidic wines. For taste, the pH level of the acidity is crucial. Wines with a low pH value have a more concentrated acidity, in contrast to high pH levels, which create a lesser, weaker or very mild acidic taste. The pH value for neutral tasting (barely noticeable) acidity is about 7 – the same as water. Mild acidity in wines often results from a second, malolactic fermentation, during which lactic acid bacteria transform a portion of the tarter malic acids into milder lactic acids.

With the help of modern analytical methods, particularly gas chromatography, more than 900 substances – beyond the dominant components acids, sugar, alcohol, tannins and minerals – have been discovered in wine. Most of these are volatile aromatic substances, particularly higher alcohols. They are of course only present in very low concentrations (about 0.8 to 1.2 mg per litre), yet they have a strong influence on the aroma and taste of wine.

Sulphur dioxide is the most prominent of the components added during wine processing. Depending on sweetness and alcohol content, the amount of this element – which is necessary for extending storage life, clarity and colour – can range between 80 mg per litre in fully fermented wine to about 260 mg per litre for wines with a high residual sugar content – the highest value permitted in the EU. For *Trockenbeerenauslese* wines (medium to full-bodied dessert wines made of grapes shrivelled by *Botrytis cinerea,* or noble rot), up to 400 mg per litre is permitted. Non-sulphured wines tend to oxidise rapidly. With the use of modern technology in winemaking, the necessity of adding sulphur dioxide – to dry wines has recently been reduced. In the EU, sulphured wines must be labelled "contains sulphites" (not to be confused with sulphides).

Wine assessment

All information about the composition of wine can be retrieved by physicochemical analysis and sensory evaluation. But the data provided by analysis has little to say about the excellence and character of a wine. These values are obtained by wine tasting, during which the features picked up by our senses play a central role.

The colour of wine derives primarily from the pigments in grape skins. In white wines, these are the flavonals; with reds, the anthocyanins. As a kind of pigmented tannin – also called oenin – they belong, along with the other tannins, to the phenolic compounds. Their non-volatile substances combine with the yeast to deepen the colour of wine. Along with the respective characteristics of grape varieties, the colour of wine is determined by the typical ripening of the vintage on the vine, cellar processing and length of bottle storage, which makes red wines increasingly lighter and white wine deeper in colour.

Clarity also plays a large role in the visual image of wine. Cloudiness is an obvious sign of poor quality. The neutral-tasting crystals of sediment that sometimes form on the cork or at the bottom of the bottle when it has been exposed to great differences in temperature are usually acid precipitates. Although they do not affect the quality, they can usually be prevented by stabilising the wine sediment. Equally, the tannin sediment that can develop in older red and port wines has no immediate effect on taste. Careful decanting can help keep these perceived flaws in the bottle. Other visual characteristics of the composition of the wine include its fluidity (leaving, for example, "legs" or "tears" in the glass) and its carbonation, which particularly in sparkling wines manifests in the kind and duration of the bubbles it makes.

Smell and taste wield a strong influence in the quality assessment, which is chiefly determined by aromas. Primary aromas evolve with the grape's metabolism on the vine, the development of which varies according to climate and ripeness. Secondary aromas emerge during grape processing, must treatment and fermentation. Tertiary aromas arise during barrel storage (for example, maturation in oak barrels) and in bottles.

As previously described in the section on wine analysis, sugar (saccharose), acids, minerals and

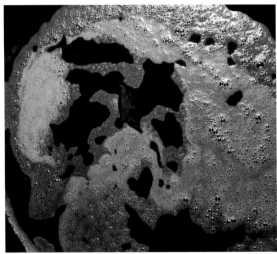

Left: Autumnal vineyards in the central Rhineland near Bacharach-Steeg (Germany).
Top: Glass airlocks (Nessler's fermentation lock filled with water or glycerol) provide an airtight seal on the fermentation tanks, through which, however, the carbon dioxide created during fermentation can escape.
Above: Red wine must from pressed, macerated grapes. Solid substances, particularly from the grape skins and seeds, dissolve into the liquid and influence the character and taste of the wine, mostly through their tannins, pigments and aromas, depending on the length of fermentation.

trace elements, tannins (polyphenols), sulphuric acids and higher alcohols – particularly glycerol – are determining factors for the taste composition of wine. Alcohol is only an indirect taste medium that supports the character and richness of the wine (its "body").

Positive and negative characteristics can be associated with each individual criterion for different wines. Wine flaws are often based on microbiological transformations during wine processing, such as cloudiness caused by yeasts or proteins, or alteration of colour due to oxidation. Some flaws in wine can be detected by smell as well as taste, such as a tinge of vinegar or lactic acid. Development in an impure barrel can lead to a musty smell. Another smell that is a sign of flawed wine is a "rustic" or geranium smell, which is caused by lactic acid bacteria. "Corked" wine, on the other hand, isn't really a flaw of the wine but the result of a musty cork. Wines that have been stored and matured for a long time often develop a special aroma, called "bouquet", that is reminiscent of a crust of bread. Even when the colour of these usually sweet white wines resembles that of sherry, these are especially prized for their impressive bouquet.

Wine tasting

In order to gain an impression of the quality of the wine, a "sensory examination" is necessary, during which each individual distinguishing characteristic mentioned above must be critically evaluated. In working professionally with wine, this sensory tasting is essential, while social wine tastings for entertainment are often simply hedonistically motivated popularity contests for the consumer. Although subjectivity cannot be ruled out, proper professional wine tastings are based on basic tenets that lead the examiner to the most dependable, objective results possible. During the oenological, empirical examination of the product, organoleptic assessment is of equal value to commercial considerations, such as the purchase of wine or the assessment of its shelf life and gastronomic suitability (as an accompaniment to particular foods).

The various methods used in the practice of testing and assessing wine assume that the assessor has the necessary knowledge and experience. Almost all wine assessments are conducted using the senses and rely on the categories of colour, smell and taste. Each assessment model can be further broken down by the secondary characteristics – such as clarity, viscosity and general impressions (harmony, typicality, etc). The wine taster documents his impressions by awarding points on the basis of each individual assessment system.

In order to guarantee complete neutrality regarding sensory perception, wine tastings are conducted "blind" – in other words, without knowledge of the name of the product and its creator. The wine assessment is usually based on a small amount, usually in special tasting glasses, which have a special form conducive to wine tasting. For professional wine tastings, collections of various aroma samples to get acquainted with them and an "aroma wheel", which depicts the concepts and categories of the individual attributes, provide a good basic level with which to get on-the-job training.

Wine storage

In comparison to many other beverages, wine is notable for, among other things, its long shelf life. Apart from wines that have been fortified with added alcohol (sherry, port), shelf life isn't unlimited, if a special taste experience is anticipated after a longer period of storage. Wine is a fascinating collector's item – both as an abstract and actual commodity – due to information on the label, such as vintage or origin, and its resulting unlimited variety. Traditionally, technical and physical requirements are associated with proper storage which, thanks to modern cellar technology, no longer needs stringently to observe the caveats of previous centuries. In particular, wines intended for early consumption can more easily be handled without the danger of a noticeable loss of quality.

At the same time, when storing wine, it is advisable to take into account that wine is a fragile product, the development of which is by no means completed when it is bottled. The complex maturation and ageing processes proceed very differently. They are dependent on microbiological factors

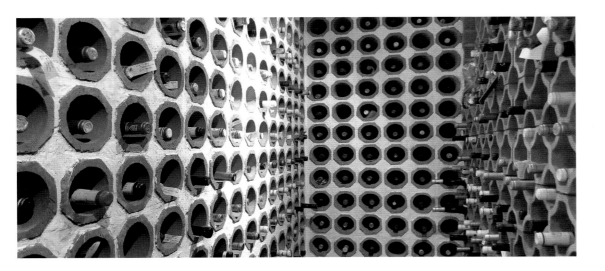

such as the influence of phenols (with red wines) and acids (particularly with white wines) but also physical influences (storage temperature). The three classic recommendations for proper storage are focused on wine's ageing process:

- Storage at a constant temperature (white wines at 8°-12°C, red wines up to 16°C) and humidity (60 per cent to a maximum of 80 per cent) in an odourless environment with minimum vibration.
- Bottles with corks should be stored horizontally or slightly tipped so that the cork remains elastic and refrains from drying out. This doesn't apply to spirits or to wine bottles sealed with synthetic materials, glass or screw tops.
- Appropriate lighting that isn't too strong, such as LED with little heat generation.

There is a broad range of appliances, tools, shelving and accessories available to satisfy the logistical, physical and design needs of commercial wine sellers and collectors for optimum storage and presentation. Before deciding which particular storage and presentation technology or accessories to buy, the questions of the location's conditions, the necessary capacity requirements and modification and expansion possibilities (flexibility of mode and construction) should be taken into account.

The array and diversity of racks for the display and storage of wine bottles has recently reached a level of flexibility and mobility, including practical materials and attractive design features, that can hardly be surpassed. The classic remains the functional rack made of diverse kinds of wood. Metal racks – useful because of their stability and resistance to high humidity – are particularly suited to installation in damp cellars. Wine racks made of synthetic materials are quite stable despite their lightweight material. Elaborate ceramic racks not only suit the ambience but are also porous and very resistant to pressure. Racks made of black, natural igneous rock, tuff or cast stone made to look like sandstone make an imposing impression. Masonry racks look both rustic and decorative.

There is a diverse range of appliances that create the perfect climate for wine storage. They range from wine refrigerators that feature climate control and variable capacities (up to about 4,000 bottles) to soundproofed climate-control coolers. They can guarantee a stable temperature between 10°C and 12°C. Humidifiers can help achieve a constant humidity in wine cellars, and some models even remove unpleasant odours.

Opposite page: In professional wine tastings, wine colour is the first indication of age and character.
Above: Drainage pipes set in plaster enable an ideal temperature and humidity for wine storage. This system is particularly suited to storing individual bottles. Labels on the neck of the bottles carrying information about the individual wines make it easy to find what you're looking for without having to move the bottles out of their resting places.

The presentation of wine

The excitement of purchasing and enjoying wine is influenced by a combination of stimulation, information and experience. The requirements for this are product quality, personal consultation and an ambience that meet the expectations of the customer and guest. Architectural design – whether of a new or renovated old building – and associated activities have no small influence on the image and profile of an establishment and its products and services. This realisation has led to a transformation in all areas of wine marketing – whether for direct sellers, dealers or restaurateurs – with diverse improvements and often striking renovations. The goal is always to optimise the presentation of wine and give the visitor a complete experience.

The planning process must first involve identifying business considerations such as financing, location, area, building, customer target group, capacity and personnel. The builder and architect develop their plans based on these economic imperatives. At the same time, other aspects such as effective use of space, product presentation, choice of materials and colour must be taken into account.

Although the functionality of the spaces is of primary importance, criteria such as individuality, clarity or aesthetics must also be addressed. As well as lighting and furnishings, the surface areas of floors, walls and ceilings create the desired room

Top left: Sales and tasting area at López de Heredia wine cellars in Haro (Spain). The exhibition pavilion designed by architect Zaha Hadid in 2002 incorporates an historic sales pavilion from 1910, thereby creating an intriguing tension between art deco and contemporary design language. Since then, the building has been integrated into the traditional complex of the 130-year-old cellars.
Bottom left: L'Intendant wine shop in Bordeaux (France). The premises is considered one of the more unusual wine shops, and not only because of its selection of about 15,000 bottles. Almost all classified Bordeaux cru wines are displayed along the 12-metre, spiral staircase, designed in 1990 by Paris architects Jean-Francois Bodin and Jean-Michel Rousseau.

This space-defining architectural element has since been copied many times. In 2009 Jean-Michel Rousseau redesigned it.
Right: Enoteca Italiana in Siena (Italy). This wine shop was originally designed in 1933 to be a display for Italian wine production and was established in 1950 in the former Medici fortress. The permanent display contains more than 1,500 wines from 600 producers. The Enoteca is considered to be the predecessor of many similar regional and local establishments for tastings and information. The displays integrated into the racks contain information about various wine-producing regions, vintners and wines.

atmosphere. Materials used to accent the overall impression are essential to the image created. This applies to all elements and areas of a project, with diverse materials offering innumerable variations and design possibilities. Natural materials from the immediate environment are usually preferred for making "wine-friendly" spaces – natural stone, slate or quarry tile for floors, for example, which emphasise the identity of the interior design for the "leading actor": the wine. Materials that mirror vineyard terrain, such as local stone or wooden barrels, enhance the authenticity of the ambience. Ceilings and walls that either harmonise or contrast in structure and colour also have a decisive effect on the general impact of the design.

The "feel-good factor" of a space for customers and guests is determined not only by the furnishings and materials but also by its colour. Studies on colour psychology have yielded generally accepted knowledge about the often unconscious effect of colour and how it creates a sense of attraction or rejection in the beholder. Colour symbolism can be useful in choosing a colour scheme. Light colours such as oranges and yellows stand for sensations of warmth and light, levity and cheerfulness, freshness and enjoyment. Depending on the shade, brown can symbolise dignity, rustic life, tradition and closeness to nature; and dark red gives a sense of warmth, stillness, solemnity and stability. Colour and lighting concepts should, if at all possible, encompass not only the sales areas but also the entire establishment.

Wine sales at source
Wine estates, vintners' associations and wine cellars that sell their products directly to consumers have recently seen their sales become of central importance to their business activity. In order to meet higher expectations of product and service and offer flexibility in choosing where to purchase, as well as accommodate the transforming customer demographic and the increasing customer interest in wine, the formerly standard wine cellar tour, accompanied by a tasting in a rather simply decorated tasting room, is no longer sufficient. As a consequence, numerous changes – often coupled with a shift in ownership or family generation – have come into force, including investment in production and storage areas and meeting space requirements to optimise (bottled) wine sales to the consumer with direct marketing.

As soon as an appropriate change of focus has been determined, the next step – as is usual with building projects – is to conduct a critical analysis of the entire structural and technical situation of the existing buildings. For this, the geographical situation of the wine estate is examined in light of its marketing aspects (for example, location and accessibility to potential customers). In contrast to the building considerations of other types of wine marketing, such as specialised shops or restaurants, structural changes to the wine estate itself are generally closely linked to other renovation and expansion measures. These can include production and administration

as well as living space. Within the context of the growing potential of wine tourism, it is advisable also to consider possible extensions to transport and plumbing, for example, or include the building of a hotel.

Thanks to the possibility of financial support from the EU for building wine estates, there is a bit less pressure on the obligatory cost-effectiveness calculations, and the boom in wine gastronomy at wine estates makes a relatively early return on investment a distinct possibility. At the same time, the realisation of all plans at once only rarely succeeds. Therefore a professionally backed plan should also take into account potential future building phases and a need for extra space to accommodate new buildings. If it is possible to achieve the proposed alterations within the scope of a new building project, the outcome will generally become more harmonious and deliver more satisfactory results. Making potentially difficult compromises that are often caused by renovation and extension will not be necessary, such as those deriving from having to add new sales and tasting areas to old buildings.

A style clash can hardly be avoided without clear ideas about the general image of the establishment. In creating a building for selling wine, there are generally three options:

• Effective architectural contrast, achieved by integrating modern architecture with the existing conventional building style of the structure and its interior.

- Predominance of traditional architectural elements in the – potentially renovated – existing building, both externally and internally.
- Consistently contemporary architecture, style and image in both external and interior design.

Other principal aspects – such as the distinctive character the entire project should have – are closely tied to the search for a solution that is defensible both financially and with regard to staffing. Should a streamlined, perhaps minimalist style be given priority, or a decorative, representative style that aims to impress? And, concerning corporate identity, is the visitor's visual impression of the wine shop or tasting area authentic and consistent with the image of the producer and their wines? In the end, the question of future acceptance of the architecture and its interior design remains – it could in later decades appear outmoded. Ideally, however, it should continue to be seen as timeless and attractive.

In comprehensive planning for renovation and rebuilding, it is often possible to integrate parts of the production areas – such as the barrique storage – in the sales areas. Separated only by transparent glass elements in the floor or walls, the combined view of wine ageing in the cellar and the product display in the bottle can be fascinating. Larger cellars, where a visitors' programme is often professionally organised, can offer guests an extensive panorama, with a wine sales area located on a passageway that intermittently opens out to afford a view of the production process. Setting the stage for wine takes place here "on stage", as it were.

As functional furnishings, display walls and racks, counters, tables and chairs comprise the central elements of a wine boutique, whether it is intended only for tasting or also for serving food to guests. The choice and placement of design elements should be based on the basic purpose of the wine shop to offer an experiential fulfilment of demand. For this, it is important during early deliberations to remember that every design element must, alongside its importance as a useful object, also serve a decorative purpose. Examples of this are information displays, backlit presentation walls, unusual wine racks made of various materials or display cases with rare wines or specialities of the estate.

Different kinds of seating can also serve as focal points – whether as cubes, benches, barstools, designer or lounge furniture – inviting people to linger. As well as tables of various sizes and materials, seating should be tailored to its respective functions, depending on whether it is purely designed for wine tasting or an expanded food menu in an adjoining tavern. For food service – which has to follow special regulations in wine establishments – the building plans must include additional, requisite spaces (kitchen, sanitary facilities). Seating flexibility is particularly relevant when attracting customers through cultural or other events at the wine estate. Concerts, exhibitions, lectures and readings have recently become a regular feature on the programmes of many wine estates.

Wine gastronomy

As with wine production, a striking heterogeneity also exists in the business of wine gastronomy. Most important for the respective orientation of these diverse venues is the kind of public one wishes to attract. This serves as a guideline for the "software", such as the combination of assorted drinks and menus, and "hardware" – in particular, space allocation, which may include additional rooms for wine sales, in-house events or rentals. The respective ambience of a given wine restaurant should determine its general and individual, venue-specific features. Depending on the kind of venue, a wine bar can feel unconventional, unpretentious or chic; a wine bistro, authentic, cosy or traditional; and a gastronomic "house of wine", sophisticated and elegant. The wide variety of terms for wine gastronomy venues – from the Mediterranean cantina to traditional tavern – highlights the colourful mix of traditional wine cellars, wine restaurants with national and regional emphases and gourmet restaurants with an exceptional selection of wines. In some countries, for example in southern Europe and German wine-producing areas, traditional wine restaurants are a dominant feature, while in other regions – particularly in urban areas – the wine venue sector is enlivened by creative variety. Wine taverns with their atmosphere of dark wood interiors – an unchanging fixture across the centuries – are cultural monuments of past epochs. Wood still serves as a design element in

Wine estate PoderNuovo in Palazzone, San Casciano dei
Bagni (Italy). The southern Tuscan estate was built in 2009
by the architects Alvisi Kirimoto + Partners according to
sustainable strategies. The cubature of the building orien-
tates itself on the structure of the landscape, and geothermal
and solar energies are its power source. Owners Paolo and
Giovanni Bulgari, members of the famous jewellery and
wristwatch dynasty, saw this as a requirement for their new
building.
Looking down from the grand, 80-m² tasting area, fitted out
with rustic wooden furniture, on the second floor, you can
see the production area and the 400-m² wooden barrel
storage area with more than 160 barriques for ageing San
Giovese red wine.

Left: Specialist shop Wein & Wahrheit (wine and truth) at the wine cellars of Hoechst in Suzbach/Frankfurt (Germany). The shop has about 85 m² of sales area. It was designed by the Ippolito Fleitz Group and opened in 2011. Inspired by the idea of a library with its books, the space is covered on all sides by wines. Mirrors running along the edge of the ceiling expand the impression even further. One bottle of each wine stands upright on each narrow shelf, with the others lying horizontally behind them. The cube-shaped tasting, packing and till tables are made of light oak wood.
Near right: The material and arrangement of wine racks has been expanded in recent years in numerous ways so that there are always new design ideas and possibilities for wine

restaurants, particularly for eye-catching bottle racks and shelves for glasses that often reach to the ceiling. But integrated wine-cooling units with protective glass doors are now a vital, functional element of contemporary technical fittings. Technical equipment that can pour wine by the glass is also recommended. These can conserve the contents of open bottles for weeks and maintain beverage quality.

Wine restaurants are even more subject to changing design trends than vintners' shops and off-licences. Traditional environments used to be the leading design influence on these venues, but now clear, minimalistic design is often preferred – as demonstrated by the influx of lounge furniture, the comfort and ease of which is as useful as it is appropriate to the taste of the times. Whether classical, modern or rustic, the choice of seating arrangements should be primarily influenced by ergonomic rather than avant-garde principles: enjoying wine is a sensual experience and should include relaxation. The charm of a wine bar derives from a sophisticated combination of diverse furnishing elements, such as buffet, tables and chairs, bar stools and high tables, perhaps also a centrally placed presentation and tasting table as a further eye-catching feature.

As previously mentioned, the effect on guests of the materials used for the ceiling, floors and walls on the ambience, as well as their colour and lighting, should not be underestimated. The effective use of (usually) dimmed lighting and the necessity

shops – such as horizontal wine display, or a design that mimics the architectural structure.
Far right: Par Terre wine boutique in Landau (Germany). One of the most elaborate and innovative specialist shops in German wine regions, it was opened in the summer of 2014 along the southern Wine Route. Berlin fashion designer Michael Michalsky and Daniel Ringwald of raumKonzepter designed the display and event centre, including the lecture hall and restaurant, in a former army barracks. Light oak panel floors with 50 ornaments made from the ends of wine barrels, and a wall made of stone from the best vineyard terrain, are just some of the design elements of this well-lit shop, which boasts a selection of about 300 wines.

of a visually unhampered recognition of the product require a very careful compromise. Colour and clarity of the wine in its glass play a particularly important role in the visual experience of enjoying wine. If food is to be integrated into the service, then considerable extra effort and expense will frequently be involved in order to meet special technical and logistic criteria, depending on the quality and extent of what is to be served. Styling the rooms for patrons often requires particular kinds of renovation. Additionally, extending and redesigning the kitchen and other working spaces may become necessary. The greater the entrepreneurial commitment, the more relevant the idea of quality becomes for the guest, and particularly for the economic success of the proprietor.

Specialised wine trade

Similar planning and realisation processes are recommended for specialised wine shops, which have been subject to the same extensive sea changes as the hotel and restaurant industry. Facing aggressive competition that has access to a large self-service area, the competitive edge of the wine merchant derives from the distinctive display of his selection, personal and competent customer service and a shop design that expresses individuality. The appearance of the shopfront is more important for the wine specialist's shop than a wine discounter. Apart from the impression the shop creates from a distance, the shop window design

(created by products displayed with small design elements) also plays an important role. An attractive facade and shop entrance should reach for a certain marketing impact – and most of all reduce any hesitance a potential customer might feel about entering the shop. At the same time, structural caveats can sometimes limit the extent of the desired style.

As with the interior design of a wine shop, planning must be based on marketing strategy and architectural elements. Functional zones (customer areas, storage and staff rooms) must be determined by the arrangement and deployment of furnishings for marketing and tasting. As wine is a heterogeneous product due to its diverse origins and creation methods, and its marketing necessitates a great need for customer consultation, great care must be taken in distinguishing appropriate display areas for the presentation of each product.

The sales presentation of wine is often conducted using bright yet dignified colour schemes – frequently including wood in high-quality displays. Contrasting colour – for example, having dark racks standing in front of a light background, or the other way around – can help create a certain fluid energy in the shop. Lighting – which should be neutral in colour and warmth – can establish an atmospherically enticing effect. Achieving visual effects in individual areas can also lend support to the general display. As wine is seldom purchased spontaneously, wine tastings alongside individual consultation can positively influence purchasing intentions.

A dedicated service area with coolers for white and rosé should be available.

At the heart of the sales area, in addition to the counter, special wine racks should allow for standing or slightly tipped bottles to be presented. Further bottles of the same type of wine should be able to be stored horizontally. As bottles bearing labels that are immediately identifiable have a strong marketing effect, standing these upright is preferable. Depending on the area available, diverse furnishings and design elements, such as tables, display islands and glass cases, should enhance the basic decor. This also includes areas for special displays – such as barrels or wooden crates from Bordeaux – as well as special offers of rare wines and accessories such as glasses, wine cellar equipment and wine literature, which can enrich and individualise the shopping experience.

To further establish the profile of a wine shop, special events are useful in creating a good customer relationship. These include in-house exhibitions, wine tastings with professional commentary or wine seminars. Therefore, the designation of all the area available should allow for the possibility of such events, such as a logistics (incoming and outgoing delivery) area.

Wine section at the SPAR Flagship store in Budapest (Hungary)

Architects: LAB5 architects, Edömér utca 4,
1113 Budapest, Hungary, www.lab5.hu
Team: Linda Erdélyi, András Dobos, Balázs Korényi,
Virág Gáspár
Total floor area: 2000 m² (shop), 100 m² (wine section)
Completed: 2013
Contact: SPAR flagship store, Alkotás utca 53,
1123 Budapest, Hungary
www.mompark.hu

A white band on the ceiling with large, round downlights guides the customers to the inside of the inviting-looking SPAR flagship store in MOM Park, a mall built 15 years ago in Budapest's 12th district. A competition was announced for the redesign of the flagship store, and the winning design, by the architects at LAB5, is rather atypical for supermarkets. While the interior of the chain's supermarkets is usually dictated by the Austrian parent company, free rein was given here to the Hungarian centre management and the LAB5 team under András Dobos. The architects developed a concept in which the various product areas such as produce are clearly delineated and seem like indi-

vidual market stalls. The design of the ceiling was accorded particular significance: it links the various areas together and helps the customers to orient themselves. To achieve this, the architects opted for timber-finish HPL panels of various sizes and shapes fixed to the bare ceiling at intervals of five to eight centimetres.

In the rear area of the shop floor, one comes to the real high point of the store: the wines. Here, the ceiling transforms into a sculptural object. The ribs arc to the floor, forming shelves and tables for the presentation of the wines. Bottles are displayed both upright in neat rows on the shelves and lying on little islands that are also formed of ribs. The department has its own counter where customers can go for advice.

The lighting, too, serves an important function: the shop's entire merchandise is set in scene with downlights. Particularly in the wine department, LAB5 integrated additional hanging lamps that are shaped like wine bottles and glow from within. They serve to underline the individual character of this area. Despite the wave movement of the ribs, the regular spacing lets them radiate calm, leaving the spotlight to the wines.

Here, LAB5 have created an attractive, almost sheltering atmosphere, which András Dobos fittingly likens to a cave or a stone cellar. This showpiece store was built in a record time of around ten weeks and is soon to be followed by others – to the certain delight of the customers.

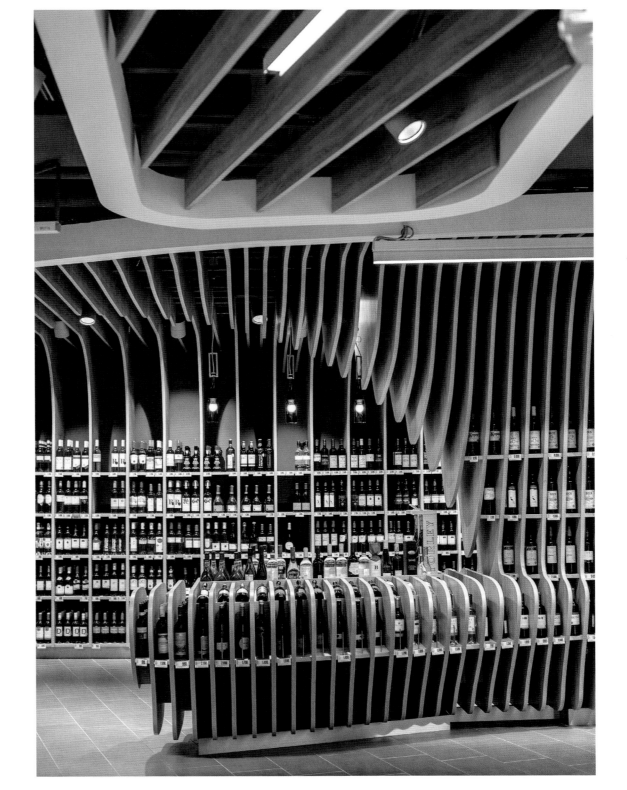

Floor plan
Scale 1:800

1 Entrance
2 Fruit and
  vegetables
3 Bakery
4 Meats
5 Wines
6 Wine information
  counter
7 Checkout

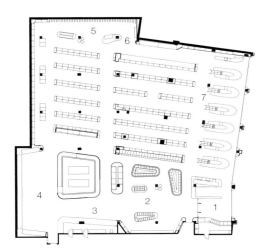

DiVino in Budapest (Hungary)

Architects: suto interior architects,
Ötvös János utcában 1b, 1021 Budapest, Hungary
www.suto.hu
Total floor area: 130 m²
Completed: 2010
Contact: DiVino Wine Bar, Szent István tér 3,
1051 Budapest, Hungary, www.divinoborbar.hu

The spaces now occupied by the DiVino Wine Bar once housed a luxury restaurant. When that closed in the wake of the economic crisis and the owner of the nearby restaurant TIGRIS was asked whether he wanted to take over the lease, he did not hesitate for long. The premises were located in the best area of Budapest, directly across from St Stephen's Basilica, and his idea was to open a wine bar there. He had become aware of the architects Kata and Laszlo Suto through their appealing design of the Drop Shop Wine Bar near the banks of the Danube River.

Their proposal for the DiVino Wine Bar left the existing room layout largely intact, but changed the atmosphere completely: black and light-coloured cedar wood now dominate the formerly white spaces. The individual planks of wood are fixed to the walls and ceilings quite visibly with black nails recalling staves. For the floors, the architects used elastic flooring that looks uncannily like raw steel plates, but that markedly damps impact sound.

Entering the wine bar, one is first struck by the long bar that extends all the way to the rear of the room. While the cube is also clad in cedar wood, the upper part of the bar area is executed in exposed concrete – a material for which the architects have a "weakness", as Laszlo Suto puts it. Featuring bottle shelves reminiscent of wine crates, as well as standing tables and bar stools, the front area immediately adjacent to the entrance has the feel of a wine shop. This impression changes as one goes

further back: low tables, also of cedar wood, and stools complement the long, high-backed bench along the side wall as well as the lounge seating islands. The lighting changes accordingly: while the entrance area, lit directly from above, is bright, the indirect wall lighting in the rear area makes the space appear deliberately dark, calling attention to the chandeliers, which were made especially for this bar. The lighting of the bar counter is particularly striking, featuring a lamp designed by the architects themselves. It not only has a functional purpose, but is also meant to promote brand recognition: the DiVino wine bar concept is being franchised throughout Hungary.

There is an impressive selection of wines on offer, with some 140 Hungarian wines available by the glass. This is the heart of the DiVino concept: a clear focus on domestic wines made by young, up-and-coming vintners, each of whom presents his products on one evening a week on a rotating basis. The moderate prices and the opportunity to buy the sampled wines directly at the bar make this a particularly popular choice with young patrons between the ages of 25 and 35. And if tables are impossible to get after 9 p.m., and if, in summer, more than 500 guests can be found enjoying their glass of wine in the large square in front of the bar, what better proof that this is a business idea whose time has come?

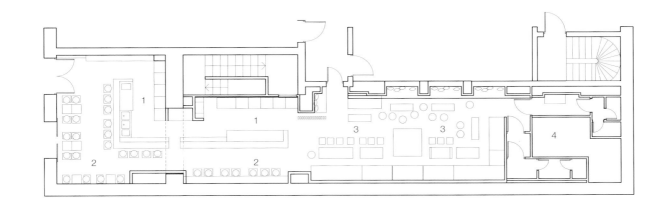

Floor plan
Scale 1:200

1 Bar
2 Bar area
3 Lounge
4 Storeroom

Balthazar Wine & Coffee Bar in Sint-Truiden (Belgium)

Architects: Creneau International, Hellebeemden 13,
3500 Hasselt, Belgium, www.creneau.com
Team: Simone Pullens, Andrew Theunissen, Joris Put,
Fre Lemmens
Total floor area: 100 m² (ground floor/bar),
30 m² (lower level), 18 m² (upper level)
Completed: 2012
Contact: Balthazar Wine & Coffee, Grote Markt 52,
3800 Sint-Truiden, Belgium,
www.barbalthazar.wordpress.com

In the southern part of the Flemish province of Limburg, nestled in the fertile, fruit-growing Hesbaye region, lies the picturesque town of Sint-Truiden.

Visitors to the Balthazar wine and coffee bar need to keep their eyes open in order not to miss the narrow entrance to this true gem. Traversing the anteroom, which is open to the street and contains rough wooden benches on which patrons can sit and enjoy a glass of wine, one arrives at the subtly lit, cosy bar area.

The bar is located on the left side of the tunnel-like interior. Behind it, a small room opens up, simple tables inviting the visitor to sit and have a glass of wine or a bite to eat.

The owner, Maurice Vroonen, worked in fashion for a number of years, operating a boutique in Sint-Truiden. He inherited his passion for wine from his father, who imported wine and dreamed of opening up his own wine bar. After turning his back on textiles, the son turned the father's dream into reality. The plans for the fit-out of the bar were drawn up in collaboration with the Creneau architecture and design practice, based in nearby Hasselt. The lead-ing designers were Simone Pullens, Andrew Theunissen and Joris Put.

The idea was to create a lively meeting place for local aficionados and tourists alike, one that was to appeal especially to young people. It is particularly among young consumers in Belgium, a traditional beer country, that interest in wine is steadily rising. The bar has 40 non-sparkling wines and 30 sparkling wines on offer, serving a rotating selection of six of them by the glass. Every day, there is a new menu with little dishes and tapas made of regional products.

The rural nature of the region is mirrored in the details of the furnishings: hunting trophies are mounted on the walls, and pheasants, hams, sausages and garlic ropes hang suspended over the bar. Preserved fish, birds and butterflies are displayed under glass domes or in frames. The atmosphere is cosy but not rustic. All interior design elements have been kept deliberately simple. The floor is simply polished concrete; the bar is made of untreated oak. All surrounds are of dark steel. The walls in the bar area are clad in a shiny brocade wallpaper, the ceilings in a stucco wall-

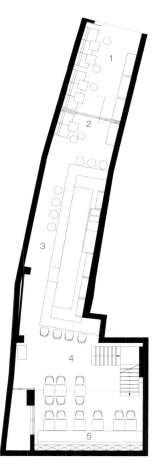

Floor plan
Scale 1:200

1 Anteroom
2 Entrance
3 Bar
4 Restaurant
5 Wine shelves

paper reminiscent of weathered metal. The shelves behind the bar consist of stackable wine crates festooned with mesh doors; they resemble the typical mesh netting found in pantries.

The rear room has been kept simple. The concrete floor continues here, but the walls are rendered and painted in a matte sand-coloured finish. Overhead hang black metal lamps of the kind one would find in a cellar or barn.
At the end wall, there is a climate-controlled cupboard for the wines above a satin-covered, vintage-style upholstered bench that extends from wall to wall. A steel staircase leads down to the sanitary rooms, where soft music plays. Over the square, white washbasins, the mirrors are let into the bottoms of horizontally sectioned wine barrels, from which the water taps protrude. Though reduced and functional, everything still references wine and agriculture.

Balthazar Wine & Coffee Bar was opened in 2012. In its original sense, "balthazar" refers to a wine or champagne bottle with a 12-litre capacity.

According to the concept jointly developed by the owner and the architects, quality wines and local products should be enjoyed in an atmosphere that typifies the region and that is cosy but not stuffy. Purist and rustic elements have been deftly woven into this unusual wine bar.
The bar is enjoying growing popularity with visitors. The "Apéro", over which locals like to meet after work, has become a sort of institution here. Parties and small concerts are regular events as well. And Vroonen is already planning to expand into the vacant shop next door.

RED Pif in Prague (Czech Republic)

Architects: Aulík Fišer architekti, Na Václavce 3b,
150 00 Prague 5, Czech Republic, www.afarch.cz
Team: Jakub Fišer, Petra Skalická
Completed: 2010
Contact: RED Pif, Betlémská 9, 110 00 Prague 1,
Czech Republic
www.redpif.cz

Wines, natural wines from France in particular, are the passion and livelihood of Milan Bartoš, owner of the RED Pif restaurant in Prague. After years of visiting France as a wine aficionado, he has been importing French wines and selling them to private clients for some 15 years.

In 2010, Bartoš decided to open up his own restaurant and wine bar. He selected a darkish corner shop to the south of the centre of Prague and hired his friend, the architect Jakub Fišer, to do the refurbishment. Fišer, whose specialisation is actually in public buildings and office blocks, took a look at the pictures Bartoš showed him of French bistros in Provence and southern France, and with his colleague Petra Skalická decided they were not transferable to Prague, nor did they characterise the personal style of the owner. Given free rein by the client, they built on the idea of natural wine as an untreated product, developing a design concept characterised primarily by the use of materials left in their natural state.

In the course of the renovation work, old wall panels were removed, exposing decades' worth of layers of render underneath – a "memory of the space", as Fišer puts it. The architects and client decided to leave this render intact, simply filling in

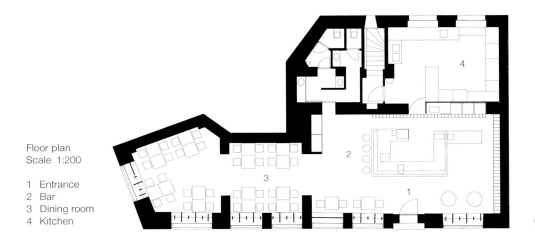

Floor plan
Scale 1:200

1 Entrance
2 Bar
3 Dining room
4 Kitchen

missing pieces and partly reapplying it. Implementing this plan, though, turned out to be trickier than foreseen, as five different colours as well as spraying, wiping and sponge application techniques were required to emulate the effect that had evolved over decades. In the bar area, the display shelves for the wine were built of mild steel. The large bar counter, the entire floor and the window sills are of rustic, oiled oak.

The indirect lighting via cove luminaires in the suspended ceiling makes for a pleasant, warm glow, which is contrasted by the soberer feel of the bare light bulbs hanging from the ceiling.
The large window areas let daylight into the bar and create a link to the exterior space. To be able to adjust the amount of light streaming in as needed, the architects developed a distinctive spatial shading element. Their idea was born as they opened a wine carton: the order in which the wine bottles were packed inside inspired them to design six almost window-high oak-lined panels shaped like wine bottles. These panels are hung on a metal rail and rest on spikes so that they can be turned as needed or even pushed entirely to the side.

Wines can be sampled at the bar or ordered to accompany food at the restaurant. The client and the architects together have created a space uniquely suited for a lovely evening over glasses of first-rate natural wine.

28°–50° Marylebone in London (United Kingdom)

Architects: B3 Designers, 302 Metropolitan Wharf,
70 Wapping Wall, London E1W 3SS, UK,
www.b3designers.co.uk
Completed: 2012
Contact: 28°–50° Wine Workshop & Kitchen Marylebone,
15–17 Marylebone Lane, London W1U 2NE, UK,
www.2850.co.uk

In London, French master sommelier Xavier Rousset and Icelandic top chef Agnar Sverrisson are living their dream of excellent gastronomy.

The suggestive name 28°–50° refers to the band of latitude within which wine is grown and produced. In the heart of the lively British capital, Rousset and Sverrisson have opened three distinctive restaurants and wine bars with a new twist on the combination of food and wine. Whether dining à la carte or dropping in for a quick drink or bite, one invariably experiences flawless and friendly service in a relaxed and stylish atmosphere. All three locations can be booked for private events as well, and offer cookery courses, workshops, tasting menus and wine seminars. In addition to a regular menu, there is a changing selection of fresh, seasonal dishes. The wine menu contains some 30 carefully selected items – and if one is disinclined to follow one's own intuition in the selection of the right wine accompaniment, the knowledgeable staff is happy to help out.

28°–50° Maddox Street, located in the middle of exclusive Mayfair, offers French bistro fare with suitable wines served by the glass, bottle or carafe. On the first floor, patrons can enjoy reasonably priced small dishes. The champagne bar, located on the lower level, serves more than 40 different champagnes. The little terrace in front of the entrance is an inviting place to watch the goings-on in the street. The spacious basement can be booked for parties.

28°–50° Fetter Lane, in the City of London, offers more than 30 selected wines as well, accompanied by small, French-inspired dishes or exquisite cheese, ham or sausage specialities.

May 2012 saw the opening of what was then the second restaurant: 28°–50° Marylebone, which complements the two wine bars. The trapezoid-shaped restaurant is found on the ground floor of a building right on the corner of Marylebone Lane and Jason Court; one enters the generous space

Floor plans
Scale 1:200

1 Reception
2 Bar
3 Wine crate shelf
4 Coat rack / office
5 Wine cellar
6 Storeroom
7 Kitchen

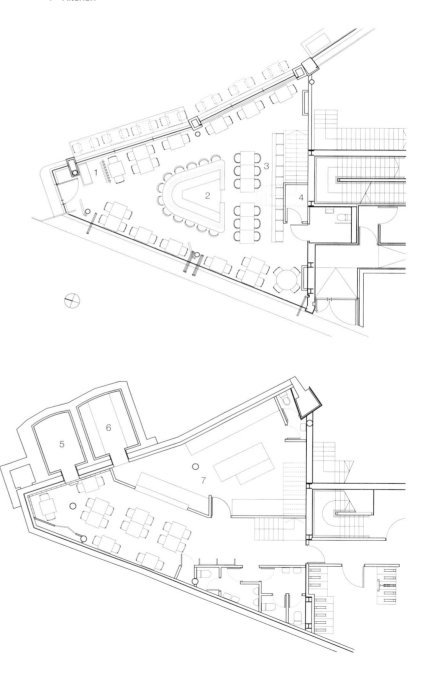

through an entrance on the narrowest side. Rousset and Sverrisson entrusted the interior refitting and furnishing to the planners at B3 Designers, a practice specialising in hotel and restaurant design. Architect Mark Bithrey set himself the task of making optimal use of space and light in the lofty, almost triangular restaurant. His job was made easier by the windows on the long sides of the building, which are open to the streets and let lots of daylight into the ground floor.

The interior is a symbiosis of solid, vintage-style elements befitting the charming 19th-century building, and light, modern touches. Unsurprisingly, oak, an important feature in wine production, plays a central role in this meeting place for wine aficionados. Solid oak parquet was chosen for the floors, and rough, grey-brown boards for the walls. The bistro tables and chairs by the windows are also made of wood. Playing off against the warm colour of the oak are the other elements, most of which sport cool hues such as white, blue and silver. The pièce de résistance on the ground floor is the U-shaped bar, placed right in the middle of the space and clad in white ceramic tiles. Above it hangs a U-shaped steel structure that echoes the shape of the bar. Lamps are incorporated into its lattice-like struts, but it also serves as a hanging rack for wine glasses, in which the light is reflected and multiplied to great effect. Struts of matte metal suspend the structure, which is made of the same material, from the white-varnished wooden ceiling. Ventilation and water pipes of zinc were deliberately left exposed. In combination with the plain metal hanging lamps, they lend the place an industrial feel. Blue, floor-mounted bar stools with matte black iron columns are arranged around the curve of the bar.

A special atmospheric element behind the bar is a ceiling-height steel shelf that holds the wine bottles in drawers made of wine crates. A rectangular recess contains refrigerators and wine cabinets

under a marble counter. Above that are more steel hanging racks for glasses. Another attractive feature is the room divider made of the sides of a riddling rack, located right at the entrance. Mirrors of various sizes and with various frames reflect the light and enlarge the room while making for a homely atmosphere.

The London wine bar looks light and airy; old and new elements complement each other perfectly. The sophisticated lighting and the light reflexes from the mirrors and glasses play off beautifully against the combination of warm-hued wooden elements with cool spots of colour – like those in the bar, the bar stools and the steel used – resulting in an impression of luminous clarity.

The lower level, which contains the open kitchen and the restaurant, is reached via a staircase of rough oak board, illuminated sparingly by simple, standard lamps. At the bottom, one finds oneself not in a dim basement, but in a warmly lit, cosy space in which various elements from the level above, such as the white tiles on the wall, the bistro furniture and the mirrors, are echoed. Patrons who prefer a more intimate atmosphere can book a table for an à la carte meal here.

A sommelier is in charge of the wine list, which usually features 15 open wines and a further 15 that can be ordered only by the bottle. The different menus for the restaurant and the wine bar both offer culinary delights. Naturally, the same care as in the other two bars is taken with everything.

28°–50° Marylebone offers regular wine workshops. In addition, one can also book wine tastings led by the sommelier, who shares a lot of useful knowledge. This wine bar in the centre of London is a great place to enjoy excellent wines and quality cuisine in a relaxed atmosphere.

28°–50° Fetter Lane
140 Fetter Lane, London EC4A 1BT, UK
www.2850.co.uk/fetter

It all began in 2010: Agnar Sverrisson and Xavier Rousset opened their first jointly owned restaurant in the City of London's Fetter Lane. They themselves designed the entire interior fit-out, whose warm, almost rustic charm mirrors the environment. In Fetter Lane, the friends achieved their dream of a restaurant in which the wine would have the same significance as the food. In the very first year, they earned a Michelin Star, which they have successfully defended to this day.

28°–50° Maddox Street
17–19 Maddox Street, London W1S 2QH, UK
www.2850.co.uk/maddox

After their successful collaboration on the Marylebone location in 2012, Agnar Sverrisson and Xavier Rousset once again turned to the interior designers at B3 Designers for their next venture. Their third restaurant, 28°–50° Wine Workshop & Kitchen in the heart of London's Mayfair, was opened in 2013. Fish and seafood play a central role in this location, and the open kitchen allows guests glimpses into the creative process of food preparation.

Neue Sternen Trotte, Weingut zum Sternen in Würenlingen (Switzerland)

Architects: Liechti Graf Zumsteg, Stapferstrasse 2,
5201 Brugg, Switzerland, www.lgz.ch
Construction: Schneider Spannagel, 5312 Döttingen,
Switzerland
Total floor area: 80 m²
Completed: 2012
Wine-producing region: Lower Aare valley
Contact: Weingut zum Sternen, Andreas Meier & Co.,
Rebschulweg 2, 5303 Würenlingen, Switzerland,
www.weingut-sternen.ch

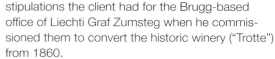

When Andreas Meier wants to get away to try his wines, he goes up a few stairs. Two steel stairways lead to the gables of the winery building. Up here, in the sensory analysis room of Weingut zum Sternen, he doesn't just have the quiet he needs, but he also has a large window that affords him a view of the goings-on up to the very borders of his property. In the midst of the other-wise dark room stands a large, white table, which is "ideal", Andreas Meier explains, "for the tast-ings, as it really allows one to address the colour of the wines." Together with his brother, Meier has been running the winery, which they took over from their parents, since 1995. The glossy finish of the table lends the reclusive room a touch of elegance. The white table was one of the few stipulations the client had for the Brugg-based office of Liechti Graf Zumsteg when he commis-sioned them to convert the historic winery ("Trotte") from 1860.

The conversion had become necessary in order to optimise the working processes on the 11.5-hec-tare vineyard and to accommodate a wine-tasting bar. This involved an almost complete razing of the old building, save for the existing cargo lift. The new build, which was completed in August 2012 after a construction period of just six months, fits into the tradition of historic barns in a rural context, both in terms of its shape and its choice of materials. In addition to a distinctive gable facade, the building sports two canopy roofs that extend far out to the front. The ends of hori-zontal drainpipes attached to the side of the roof were bent in the historic shape of the traditional quarter-sphere. The vertical drainpipe on the side was formed in the once traditional shape of a swan's neck. For both, the architects found local builders with the skills to make and implement these designs. For the roof, traditional plane tiles were used.

The entrance facade is made of pine wood with black formwork of oiled plywood. The star, which is an integral part of the Weingut zum Sternen logo and symbolises its enduring commitment to quality, was incorporated into the design of the facade as a sawn-out ornament. When the lights come on inside the building, they are refracted in the open-ings, an effect that is amplified by the transparent

Site plan
Scale 1:2000
Floor plans
Scale 1:400

1 Grape presses
2 Wine shop
3 Air space
4 Fermentation tanks
5 Sensory analysis room

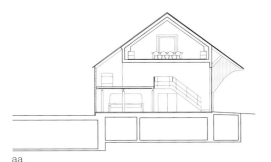

aa

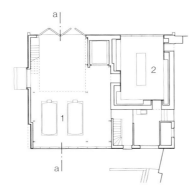

hollow boards behind the plywood. The architects had the rear facade clad in perforated plate, which gives the entire surface a sheen of calm. Here, two, hollow boards underneath protect the building from encroaching cold in winter and heat in summer, keeping the interior at a fairly constant temperature.

The design of the interior spaces is functionally arranged, allowing optimal production processes in order to help ensure the very high quality of the winery's products. The processing and vinification of the grapes takes place over three levels. Wood, OSB boards and galvanised steel constitute the dominant raw materials of the interior.

Clad entirely in black wood, the enoteca located on the ground floor links the winery with the adjoining restaurant, which is also part of the complex. The enoteca's dark design makes the room seem to retreat, ceding the spotlight to the wine. Two large hanging lamps illuminate the table top, which is made of indigenous oak and rests on four wine barrels. Lit shelves built into the wall showcase the top wines of Weingut zum Sternen and the Bessertstein cuvées created here by an association of Aargau vintners. To sample a pinot noir from the Kloster Sion vineyards in these surroundings is to realise that the architecture of the new Sternen Trotte, just like its wines, is a perfect expression of Andreas Meier's striving for the sublime.

Galerie du Vin in Zurich (Switzerland)

Architects: OOS, Hardstrasse 245, 8005 Zurich, Switzerland,
www.oos.com
Team: Andreas Derrer (co-founder),
Charlotte Malterre-Barthes (project head)
Frank Dittman, Dana al Jouder, Osama Hadeed
Lighting designers: Sommerlatte & Sommerlatte,
8037 Zurich, Switzerland
Total floor area: 120 m²
Completed: 2010
Contact: Albert Reichmuth, Feldstrasse 62,
8004 Zurich, Switzerland, www.reichmuth.ch

If you do a double take when passing the windows of Galerie du Vin in Zurich, you are not the only one. The shop might take a second to grab you, but it soon has you in its thrall. Many a curious passer-by has been drawn in by the grotto-like landscape of crates within.

The shop is the new face of a tradition-rich firm that was founded by Albert Reichmuth in 1960. The wine importer had earned much of his renown

through sales of "en primeur" from Bordeaux. To this day, Albert Reichmuth sells international wines that are true to his philosophy of "wine as an artisanal art form". The wines of his own vineyard, Mas de Theyron in Languedoc-Roussillon, are a popular staple of his repertoire. Up until recently, however, the wines could only be ordered by mail or online and picked up in the warehouse located on 145 Stauffacherstrasse in north western Zurich.

Several years ago, the idea of opening up a shop was born, a place where existing customers would be able to try wines and pick up their orders, and where new customers could be gained from among the local population.

When an old printing company on the ground floor of the firm's head office closed its doors, a spur-of-the-moment decision was taken to open up a shop there. The space now not only serves as a sales floor where some 570 wines are sold, but also functions as the Reichmuth company's calling card. The OOS architectural practice, which had a long acquaintance with the client, got the commission for the interior fit-out. As the budget was relatively limited, the idea was to create a shop-in-a-shop with a warehouse feel. From the start of their collaboration on the development of the concept, the importer and the architects agreed that the wine would not just be on exhibit in the shop, but that it would be the undisputed star and showpiece. Ultimately, the interior was clad in about 1,500 wooden wine crates, which protrude three-dimen-

sionally from the walls, the ceiling and the floor. These crates, made in the Bordeaux region, serve not only as boxes, shelves and display cases for the wines, but also as architectural elements and furniture. The wines are grouped by wine-producing region, the names of which are written on the wood. Notes bearing descriptions of the individual wines hang on a nail. The display cases, too, which are lit from within, are made from the crates; and further crates on the floor invite the visitor to have a seat.

The showroom gives the impression of a cave full of stalactites and stalagmites. Illuminating the relief structure and the wines are black, tube-like lights reminiscent of wine bottles.

The heart of the showroom is a purple sales counter, its hue chosen in homage to the grape and as a complementary colour to the wood. It is echoed in the windowsills as well.

On the other side of the corridor is a seminar room that seats about 15 people. Tastings and seminars take place here, but the room can also be booked for private purposes. The crate theme continues here on the ceiling and along one wall, where the crates also serve as a sideboard and make for pleasant acoustics.

When the wine gallery opened its doors in October 2010, all regular customers were invited to the opening. They have not been alone in appreciating the importer's new calling card, as their ranks have been swelled by a number of those who were once curious passers-by.

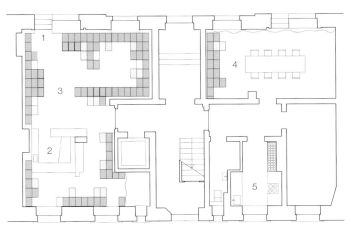

Floor plan
Scale 1:200

1 Entrance
2 Sales counter
3 Sales floor
4 Tasting room
5 Kitchen

Weingut Abril in Vogtsburg-Bischoffingen (Germany)

Architects: Wolfgang Münzing Innenarchitekt,
Neubrunnenstrasse 23, 74223 Flein, Germany
www.wolfgang-muenzing.de
Team: Wolfgang Münzing, Alfred Andelfinger,
Carolin Windisch, Christiane Spindler, Sybille Keul,
Nadine Obenland
Total floor area: 3326 m²
Completed: 2012
Wine region: Baden
Contact: Weingut Abril, Am Enselberg 1,
79235 Vogtsburg-Bischoffingen, Germany,
www.weingut-abril.de

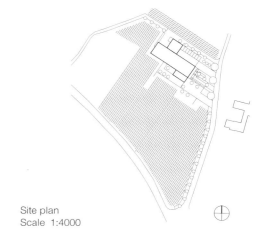

Site plan
Scale 1:4000

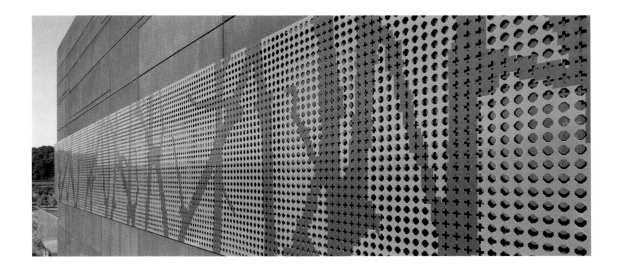

The Abril wine estate, located in the Kaiserstuhl region in the Upper Rhine plain between the Black Forest and the Vosges Mountains, was founded in 1740 and remained in the Abril family until 2006. As the then owner wanted to retire, he sold the tradition-rich wine estate to his cousin Helga Haub and her husband, Erivan. Helga Haub has known the winery since her childhood; her mother grew up here, and she herself spent several years on the property. The couple commissioned the cellarmaster Armin Sütterlin with the running and modernisation of the company. The focus of the firm had always been on the production of classic and high-quality Kaiserstuhl wines; eventually, sustainable wine production became a goal as well. In 2008, the owners completed the shift to certified organic farming methods. With its 20 hectares, the wine estate is the largest member of the national ECOVIN association. The organic certification can be seen as a further upgrading of Abril's consistently high quality.

In light of the increasing requirements pertaining to wine-growing and wine production, and the growing demand for the Abril wines, the original wine estate building in the village centre of Bischoffingen was soon bursting at the seams. A high water table, however, rendered a conversion of the traditional structure impracticable, so it was decided in 2008 to create an all-new production and sales facility for the expanding company. The right spot for this endeavour was found a bit to the west of the idyllic setting of the village, in the midst of the vineyards and at the foot of the top wine-growing location of Enselberg.

"Less is more" was the philosophy behind the planning of the new building, which was to blend respectfully and harmoniously into the surrounding landscape. A recommendation led to the selection of the designer Wolfgang Münzing, who had already made a name for himself in wine architecture. During the almost four-year period from the birth of the idea to the opening, there was regular and close communication between Sütterlin und Münzing, primarily regarding technical details. Spare, clean shapes and lines were desired. The renowned architect demonstrated great aesthetic sense in implementing the functionality that is all important in winemaking, designing a building that nestles into Enselberg. As only a two-storey cube was to protrude from the hill, the production facilities and the barrel cellar were placed underground.

The rock-like building was sheathed in rectangular plates of Cor-Ten steel, which had been weathered outside at the foundry until they had acquired their characteristic orange-red colour, a hue that gives the high-quality, rugged material a warm effect. The variously sized rectangles lend the weighty facade a kind of lightness and movement. Depending on the season, they make for an attractive contrast to the green of the vines and reference the tuff found in the area, a rock with a similar colour.

While digging the foundations, workers made an astounding discovery, coming across the remains of a 7,300-year-old village. Its inhabitants, the first food-producing peoples, made ceramics and decorated the vessels with an ornamental relief band. The epoch of this early agricultural culture is thus referred to as the Linear Pottery culture. The artefacts uncovered during the excavation – ceramic and pottery shards, bone and wood fragments – inspired a new design detail: a steel band surrounding the entire cube that pays homage to the ancient settlement. A branching vine pattern has been laser-cut into the metal. The grey base colour is interrupted by circles, the stylised brown vines by crosses, giving the band a three-dimensionality beyond that afforded by its distance to the wall. The entire building has been turned into an angular wine vessel. At the same time, the ornamental band serves a practical purpose, as it provides shade to the windows behind. Rather than dominating the vineyards, the building settles into them harmoniously. To the side, three levels of terraced flowerbeds planted with indigenous flowers and herbs echo the landscape of the Kaiserstuhl terraces.

The wine shop located on the ground floor is accessed through a pavilion of glass and steel that serves simultaneously as a foyer and exhibition hall.

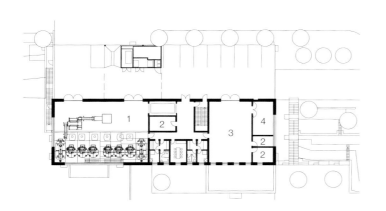

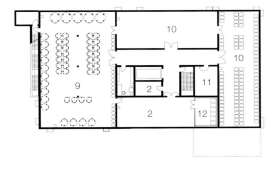

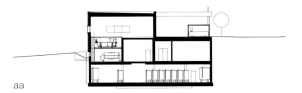

Floor plan · Section
Scale 1:800

1 Wine press room
2 Warehouse
3 Garage
4 Workshop
5 Technology
6 Heating room
7 Tastings / sales
8 Presses
9 Fermentation cellar
10 Barrel cellar
11 Wine archive
12 Cold storage

aa

The space continues to the left as an elongated rectangle. The ceiling-high windows there and the glass-fronted entrance let in a lot of daylight. The materials used include exposed concrete, stoneware and solid oak. The wall shelves and the sideboards showcasing the wines are simple rectangles of oak. Their backs are lined in dark red felt, reminiscent of red wine. These warm splashes of colour make for an inviting atmosphere and pleasant acoustics. The sparing oak furniture and the burgundy red contrast warmly with the grey of the exposed concrete, the porcelain stoneware slabs used for the flooring and the steel frames of the windows and doors. A continuous ceiling lamp extends across the entire axis of the room. In its grey-painted wooden body, dimmable warm-light tubes provide illumination that is further softened by an electroluminescent film.
Directly underneath, aligned with the lamp, is the generous counter, into which refrigerators have been built and where the wares are handed out and paid for. It is encircled by an oak band that runs parallel to the lamp above. That way, optimal lighting conditions for serving and tasting are ensured. The space behind the bar is generous; the neighbouring bottle cellar allows the customers to be served quickly and conveniently.

Visitors wishing to know more about the selection offered by the wine estate can have a seat at a long oak table in the left-hand section, also directly below the ceiling lamp. The generous space can also be booked for events. In its simplicity and openness, it offers a deferential showcase for the protagonist: the wine. Mainly vinified from indigenous varietals such as Weissburgunder (Pinot blanc), Grauburgunder (Pinot gris) and Spätburgunder (Pinot noir), the wines are grouped into the lines "Frucht" (fruit), "Stein" (stone) and "Zeit" (time). The portfolio of elegant and complex wines is rounded out by bottle-fermented sparkling wines. The Grauburgunder "Enselberg" and the Crémant are among Wolfgang Münzing's favourite wines.

With the new building came a makeover of the firm's entire corporate identity, including the launch of a new, informative homepage with an online shop. The labels of the wine bottles present themselves with the same pared-down elegance so skilfully achieved in the entire building. The efforts have paid off: since the opening, visitor numbers and turnover have both seen a boost. The festivities surrounding the opening in September 2012 went on for three days. Ever since, numerous wine lovers, tourists and architecture buffs have found their way here. And the same locals who once eyed the modern building warily now refer to it affectionately as their "Roschtkäschtle" (little rusty box).

VinoTeck, Mack & Schühle in Owen an der Teck (Germany)

Architects: UN Neugebauer Architekten, Ludwigstrasse 10,
73235 Weilheim/Teck, Germany,
www.neugebauerarchitekten.de
Total floor area: 4250 m²
Completed: 2011
Contact: Mack & Schühle, Neue Strasse 45,
73277 Owen/Teck, Germany, www.mack-schuehle.de

Teck Castle is set majestically over the village of Owen. The view of the panorama through the large windows of the new administrative tract of Mack & Schühle, one of Europe's premier wine wholesalers, is impressive. Still, the task that architect Udo Neugebauer set for himself at the beginning of the planning process in 2010 was not a simple one: namely, to unite the existing administrative building from the 1970s with the extension buildings that had gone up adjacent to it in the intervening years. The product of a collaboration with Christoph Mack, who runs the family business in the third generation, and Markus Allgaier, CFO of Mack & Schühle, the new tract was built in just one year. Neugebauer's design called for retaining the 1970s building as a "head" and attaching the new building segment directly to it. It was his express intention to leave the historically grown building complex in place as a reminder of the company's history. This entailed a partial razing of the existing hall, but parts of the concrete pillars that belonged to the loading bay were retained and integrated into the new building. The idea was to create a "lively interaction" between the new and the old, without pushing the old into the background. Most of the materials used were left in their natural state. Neugebauer speaks of the finished building as a "refined building shell".

From the outside, the building with its large glass facade looks open and transparent, a manifestation of Mack's vision of an open-minded and likeable company that puts its employees and customers first.

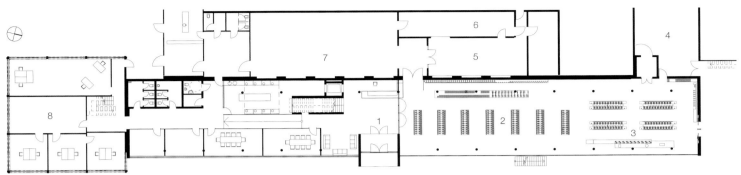

1 Entrance/reception
2 VinoTeck/wine
   shop
3 Counter
4 Incoming and out-
   going deliveries
5 BiblioTeck/tasting
   room
6 Bodega
7 Vinobar/event
   space (existing)
8 Office (existing)

To the right of the inconspicuous entrance area, one finds the wine shop VinoTeck, its name a play on the German word Vinothek and Castle Teck. About 450 wines are sold here. Despite its relative insignificance for the company's core wine business, the shop was meant to make the connection with wine as a product apparent, and to demonstrate how "modern specialised retail can work". Openness, transparency and clarity of design are evident here: glass, concrete and wood predominate. Adjacent to the shop are three spaces used primarily for customer visits, but also for events:

BiblioTeck is host to tastings, the Bodega contains selected rarities, and the VinoBar is a large event space. The dominant wall colour in all three spaces is black, suggestive of a wine cellar. In planning these spaces, Neugebauer made the deliberate decision not to include windows. The main design element is thus artificial light, which provides various moods to match the occasion.

The floor is coated in black epoxy resin. Throughout the building, there are glimpses of welded steel, as in the coatroom or in the ceiling-high bottle rack

in the Bodega. The concrete columns of the gates leading to the previous warehouse, too, were clad in steel plate and now offer a vibrant contrast both to the pine filling the gaps and to the opposite wall, which sports a brocade wallpaper of silver and anthracite.

For reasons of time and budget, the fabric of the existing administrative building was left largely intact, but its interior was completely redesigned according to Mack's wishes. It is a place of well-being for the heart of his company: his employees.

NORD Coffee · Lunch · Wine Bar in Mannheim (Germany)

Designer: Uli Odenwald, furniture I interior I design,
K 2/7, 68159 Mannheim, Germany, www.uliodenwald.com
Total floor area: 100 m²
Completed: 2013
Contact: NORD, Lange Rötterstrasse 66,
68167 Mannheim, Germany, www.nord.li

It is rare enough these days to see the wood of the wych-elm used as an interior design material in Europe, where the tree species has been decimated by Dutch elm disease. It is all the more astounding, then, to see wych-elm used in these dimensions. A 4.2 metre-long table made of the elegant, red-grained, ring-porous wood dominates the rear space of Eva Feldmann's NORD, forming a warm contrast to the walls of exposed concrete. It was Feldmann's wish to create a space in which people could come together around a table. Over it hang factory lamps from Russia. The chairs come from a school, and paintings by an artist friend adorn the walls as part of a rotating exhibition. All of these elements together give the space its personal touch.

When the owner began to turn her long-held dream of opening a cafe with a wine bar into a reality, she remembered Uli Odenwald, an acquaintance from university, whose extravagant furniture creations she had admired. The trained carpenter and designer took a number of Feldmann's ideas and suggestions on board and designed the interior in collaboration with her. There were few demands put forward by the owner, as the building had been newly constructed. Sound insulation was impor-. tant, and the central stairwell, placed cube-like in the centre of the space, was to retain its exposed-concrete look. A first draft, calling for wall-to-wall

noise insulation, was discarded for reasons of cost. As an alternative, Odenwald came up with a design in which, in every area along one side, noise-damping louvres of light spruce were placed before the existing exposed concrete wall. In the front part of the bar, the wavy benches appear to be outcroppings of this wall. Here, too, the wood stands in contrast to the otherwise exposedconcrete ceiling and rear wall, the specially made tables of composite resin panels, and the orange Charles and Ray Eames chairs. The hanging lamps, though, were created by Feldmann herself. Distributed throughout the space, cables with naked bulbs hang, spider-like, from the ceiling, bathing the room in a warm light, particularly in the evenings. To divide the space into zones, the ceiling over the bar and in the rear area was suspended and provided with a shadow gap and indirect lighting towards the exposedconcrete wall.

Above the bar counter, which is clad in raw steel plates, hang black lamps by a Danish manufacturer who produces objects by contemporary Scandinavian designers. The design is unobtrusive, ceding the spotlight to the silver espresso machine and the glass cabinet with homemade cakes.
The brass trim on the lowest section of the bar counter and on the edge of the shelves evoke the Viennese coffee house and contrast with the purist

Floor plan
Scale 1:200

1 Tasting area
2 Lounge
3 Bar counter
4 Storeroom

look of the white tiles on the wall behind, which seem more in keeping with a French bistro.

The menu features little dishes made of regional ingredients, including soups, salads and sandwiches. In the evenings, ham and cheese are served with bread as hearty accompaniments to the wine. The wine list was put together by an oenologist friend and comprises mainly wines from biodynamic cultivation as well as a few kinds of natural wine. The Mannheim wine club, which appreciates the wine knowledge to be found at NORD, holds its monthly meetings here. All the wines and the various coffees served here can be purchased for home consumption.

With NORD, Feldmann has succeeded in creating a place that perfectly unites two concepts – cafe by day, wine bar by night. No wonder the number of regular customers is high: if you've been here once, you will want to come again.

Weingut Leiss in Gellmersbach (Germany)

Architect: Michael Egger Aix Architects, Brosswalden-gasse 12, 6900 Bregenz, Austria, www.me-aix.at
Project partner: Benjamin Miatto, Kohlplatzstrasse 16, 6971 Hard, Austria, www.benjaminmiatto.com
Total floor area: 400 m²
Completed: 2011
Wine-producing region: Württemberg
Contact: Weingut Leiss, Lennacher Strasse 7, 74189 Gellmersbach, Germany
www.weingut-leiss.de

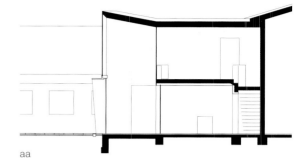

aa

Weingut Leiss lies nestled into the rolling wine-growing landscape of Württemberg. The traditional family-run company is located in the vineyards of Dezberg, where vintner Wolf-Peter Leiss has been producing classic Württemberg wines for more than 30 years.

Even though the wines were already well placed in the market and had been received favourably by the wine media, the year 2006 saw the emergence of a wish for change and development. The wines were to be given a new look, and the simple and somewhat old-fashioned wine restaurant was slated for a makeover.

Leiss and architect Michael Egger became acquainted through the vintner's sister, whose house the architect had designed. Together, the two men worked out their ideas for the design and conversion of the existing spaces. New sales and tasting rooms were to replace their slightly tired-looking predecessors, instead mirroring the winery's modern, state-of-the-art wine production facilities. With these changes, the owners wished to reach out to the next generation of customers and get their own children interested in wine growing by creating a modern company with a contemporary look. Another goal was to streamline the processes of serving the customers and patrons. Originally, the area between the residence and the warehouse and production facility contained a narrow entrance to the sales and restaurant area. In

the course of the redesign, the existing buildings were left as they were, but the nondescript entrance was replaced by a two-storey connecting building with a glass front. The sales area begins right at the entrance and extends to the newly built terrace in the rear. In case of need, the continuous space can be subdivided by means of sliding glass doors, preserving the open spatial impression that lends the new build its transparency and brightness. A purpose-made textile roller blind controls the amount of sunlight entering the glass facade. The focal point is the 6 metre-long counter of solid oak where wines are tasted and sold.

The dominant materials in the conversion are oak, glass and sandstone. The floor is of polished mastic asphalt. The solid oak shelves hold and display the wines and the liquors distilled by Leiss's father, Gerhard Leiss. A wall extending from the sales floor to the terrace is clad in variously coloured sandstone slabs from four quarries in the region. The different stones bring the colours, geology and terroir of the surrounding wine landscape indoors. Behind the wall lie facilities such as the coatroom and toilets. This area, while built into the hill, is made bright and inviting by a skylight.

The first floor contains the office as well as the gallery-like conference and tasting room. From there, one has a view down to the wine shop on the ground floor and out into the surrounding vineyards.

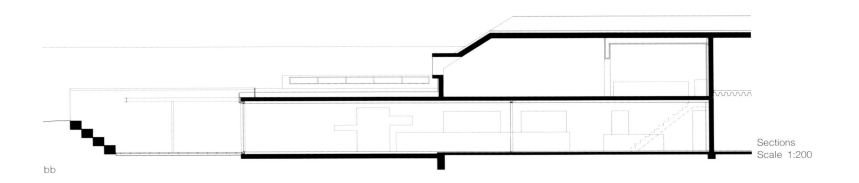

Sections
Scale 1:200

bb

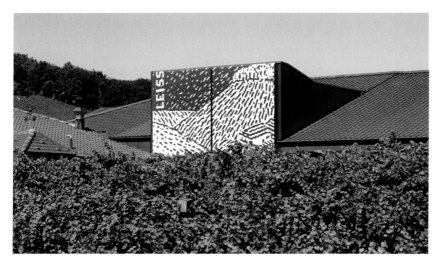

Floor plan
Scale 1:200

1 Entrance
2 Sales
3 Counter/bar
4 Wine restaurant
5 Kitchen
6 Terrace
7 Storeroom

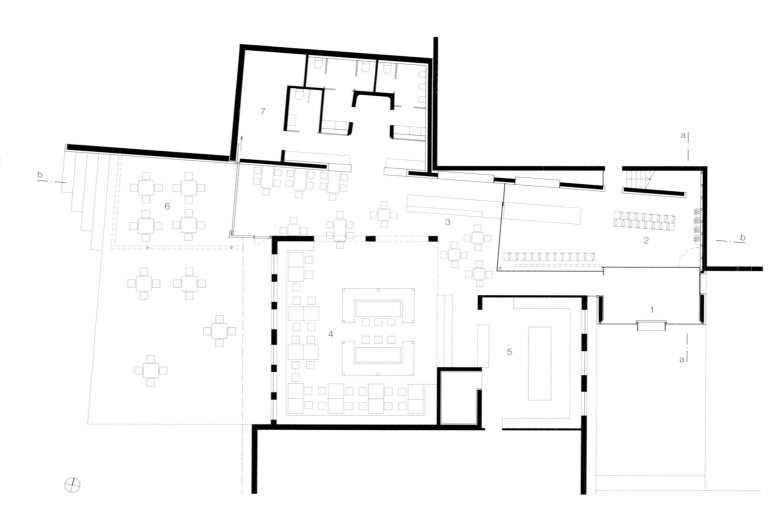

The traditional varietal of Württemberg is the Trollinger grape. The light-bodied red it produces remains a popular choice; but the character-rich, top regional wines made from the Riesling, Grauburgunder and Spätburgunder grapes are becoming increasingly significant as well. The red Lemberger bridges the connection to Egger's native country of Austria, where it goes by the name Blaufränkisch. Architecturally, the Leiss family drew inspiration from neighbouring Austria with its many newly built or rebuilt wineries, which were the trailblazers for European wine architecture.

Across from the sales counter is the original wine restaurant, which features an open pavilion in the middle of the space. Following the philosophy of pairing the old with the new, the designer kept this pavilion and clad its exterior with metal plates. These combine with the new lamps of brushed metal to contrast effectively with the old-fashioned nature of this old element. The built-in upholstered benches were given a new leather cover. The old roof beams over the generous, now bright space were preserved as well. In the open kitchen, chef Christa Leiss prepares dishes from regional ingredients to go with the house wines. The bread and cakes, too, come from the restaurant's own oven.

A large sliding glass door leads to the newly created terrace, where patrons can sit virtually surrounded by vineyards.
Thanks to the stone-clad, continuous wall, the entire newly designed sales and tasting space seems to be cut as a section through the hill. The play of the rough edges, the natural light angling in during the day and the warm, sand-coloured side light at night tell the story of the layers of soil and stone that lie beyond. The combination of sandstone and wood in purist shapes creates a modern, bright cosiness. Oak, the traditional material used in maturation barrels, is used again for the tables and chairs, but not at all in a rustic-looking way. Between the narrow wooden battens of the ceiling, dimmable matte white LED strips provide indirect lighting. The teardrop-shaped hanging lamps suspended over the counter can be dimmed as well. Even when artificial light becomes necessary, one almost has the impression of daylight.

Like the wine seminars, presentations and other events held here, the new expansion of the gastronomy and sales spaces has become part of a whole "wine experience package". From the outset, Leiss gave architect Egger free rein. Since the opening in December 2011, there has been a noticeable increase in customer and visitor numbers, particularly from wine lovers and hikers. Tourists and locals alike enjoy the new flair of the wine restaurant, flocking to the airy terrace in summer.

Weinhandlung Kreis in Stuttgart (Germany)

Designer: Furch Gestaltung + Produktion,
Leinenweberstraße 67, 70567 Stuttgart, Germany,
www.furch.tv
Total floor area: 74 m²
Completed: 2012
Contact: Weinhandlung Kreis & Krämer KG,
Dorotheenstraße 2, 70173 Stuttgart, Germany,
http://web.wein-kreis.de

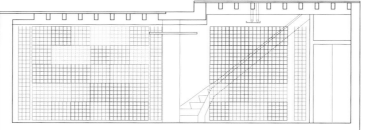
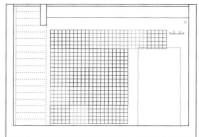

Until 2012, Weinhandlung (wine merchants) Kreis was located in the middle of Stuttgart's city centre. After a decision was made to erect a shopping centre there, it was clear that a move was inevitable. As an alternative location, owner Bernd Kreis was offered an old watchmaker's workshop that was a listed building only 100 m from his former location – and he was delighted. Here he could create a locality to reflect his own vision, something different from what he considered to be a typical wine shop. It was to be a place with a contemporary display of wine, far from the rustic ambience usually associated with the beverage. Moreover, Kreis had the idea of integrating a wine bar into his new venue in order to offer chosen wines for tasting. Particularly given his very high-quality selection, including wines that "require explaining", it was a significant sales advantage that could bring his customers closer to his products.

In Matthias Furch, the owner of Furch Gestaltung + Produktion – a combination of design firm and carpenter's workshop – Kreis found a project partner who was an avowed wine enthusiast as well as an impassioned architect. After his removal to the new premises, the previous concept of having one bottle each of his selection of 1,200 wines on display was replaced by the idea that the display and storage areas should be one and the same. "There's no warehouse. We're in the warehouse," says Kreis. After choosing a wine, the customer should be able to access it directly without a salesperson having to walk away from the sales floor to the storage area.

In stocking an average number of nine bottles per wine – Kreis's specification – 10,000 bottles needed to be accommodated – no small amount. This was a quantity that, considering the space available, made Furch dizzy. Furthermore, the owner didn't want to feature any wood, stainless steel or stone in his furnishings – all materials, he believed, of which people had seen far too much and that were all too often a focal point. According to Kreis's vision, it should be an unconventional, sober and entirely functional interior that placed the individual bottle of wine and its contents centre stage.

In order to accommodate the desired number of bottles in the 70-m² shop, the furnishing was reduced to an absolute minimum, with full advantage taken of the height of the space. Instead of racks, Furch designed a lattice grid as a vertical storage area. Like a wine's structure, the grid gave the space a structure.

Each of these "fourpointeight" racks (the name comes from the basic material: 4.8 mm-thick steel wire) could hold a total of 25 bottles in a 5 x 5 formation. But because the labels were no longer accessible to read, the designer created additional bottle holders out of bent steel platforms that could be attached to the front of the racks. In this way each rack module – including the platforms – could contain the contents of five wine cartons of six bottles each. The welded, colour powder-coated rack modules could be

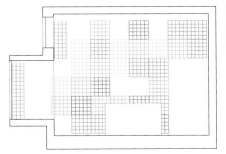
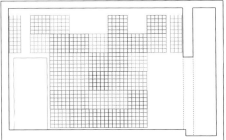
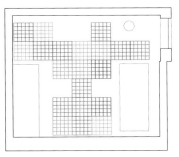

Detailed views of the walls
Lower and ground levels
Scale 1:100 (selection)

stacked up to six elements high and affixed to each other with screwed steel clamps.

In order to get the best possible fit for all kind of bottles and have them perfectly centred on the display ledges, they collected the measurements and dimensions of all bottle shapes and sizes.

The shop looks distinctive even before you enter it – the colourful grid racks can be seen gleaming through the shop windows from far away. In yellow, red, orange and white, they attract the attention of people walking by. "Even people that aren't actually interested in wine stop to look or even take photos," says Kreis. Furch didn't get his idea for the colour concept until the second attempt. The designer first considered leaving the racks in their raw steel or brass states, or chroming them. But the brass grid looked a bit like a birdcage. Nor did the chromed option look convincing. Then Furch, together with his colleague Philipp Dittus, covered the grids in bright yellow and blue varnish. They immediately recognised that this was the solution. So a palette of 18 colours and three greys was assembled – from violet, various blue and green hues mostly on the lower level to pink, red, orange and yellow hues and white on the ground floor. The colours used had, first and foremost, a design function. They consciously avoided assigning particular wines to a colour in order to maintain flexibility in their design. The mingling of the colours also brings a "certain lightness into the rooms", explains Furch.

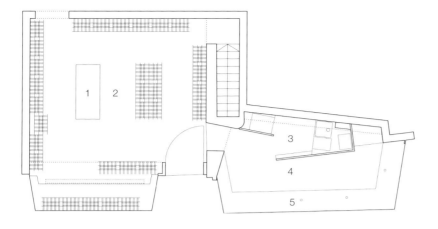

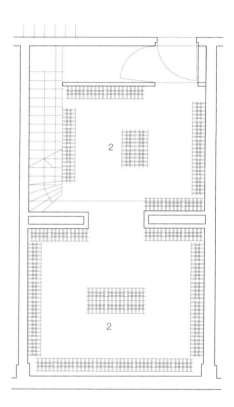

Ground level (left) and
lower level (bottom) floor plans
Scale 1:100

1   Counter
2   Sales floor
3   Wine counter
4   Bar
5   Bench

The walls are coated with dark grey, breathable plaster, which can absorb all humidity in the rooms. The dark colour of the walls makes them recede entirely behind the bright racks, which creates a sense of space. In contrast, the white epoxy resin veneer on the floor looks sober and emanates tranquillity – an effect that makes the racks even look lighter and the space larger. A leftover original, restored old wooden staircase leads into the sales floor in the cellar. There, in the absence of daylight,

the sense of sobriety is strengthened. Various light sources are combined to great effect. Large, square LED lamps with indirect light allow the two adjoined rooms to appear very peaceful. Spotlights behind the racks are directed at the dark walls, adding depth to the racks in front of them and emphasising their structure. The halogen lamps mounted over the racks on the sides of the ceiling, also painted grey, supply the necessary light for reading the labels of the wines on display and also

allow the lattice structure of the racks to reflect in the glass of the bottles. The effectiveness of the lighting concept makes the rooms emanate a sense of tranquillity that inevitably envelops customers. It is "an immersion in the world of wine", says Kreis, and a place "where wine gets the vistors' full attention".

Customers can plunge their taste buds into the wine at the new wine bar located right next to the entrance, which has a large shop window that looks out over the square. Furch and Kreis were able to create a space in a very small area – 12 m² – that can accommodate 10 to 12 people. The seating is right next to the shop window with a view to Schiller Square. It is a space for communication – guests inevitably end up chatting with one another. Kreis varies the wines available at the counter. For customers, this is an opportunity to discover new wines – and, if they like what they taste, they can purchase them. For this, Kreis selects "the more complex wines" that one wouldn't necessarily select without prior knowledge, thereby offering customers an opportunity to broaden their horizons with regard to wine. By paying a small corkage fee, customers can have any bottle they like opened for them to enjoy then and there.

One of the ways to achieve the required counter area on the minimum of space available was to resort to furnishings for sailing yachts, such as the hand sink stipulated by the office of commerce and trade. But there's still room for a record player: all day long the employees on duty select records to play. The expansive windows tempt people on the street simply to stop by. And whenever the weather allows, bar tables – built with a colourful grid structure to reflect the interior design, of course – entice guests to enjoy wine outside the shop.

With his combination of wine shop and wine bar, Kreis has created an exceptional place that appeals particularly to young people and helps them become get to know more about wine.

Wasems Kloster Engelthal in Ingelheim am Rhein (Germany)

Architects: Hille Architekten, Bahnhofstraße 23,
55218 Ingelheim, Germany, www.hillearchitekten.de
Team: Anja Rüttgers, Marcus Monreal
Interior designer: Cornelia Schroff-Graf
Lighting designer: Kai Byock
Total sales/tasting floor area: 220 m²
Completed: 2012
Wine-producing region: Rheinhessen
Contact: Wasems Kloster Engelthal, Edelgasse 15,
55218 Ingelheim, Germany, www.klosterengelthal.de

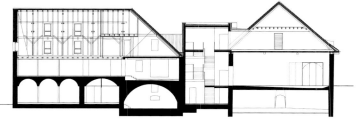

aa

In Germany's largest wine-producing area, Rhein-hessen (Rhine-Hesse), there's no shortage of innovative reconstruction and renovation of vintners' and estate shops and restaurants in recent years. Nevertheless, there aren't that many iconic architectural solutions. The "House of Wine", as the Wasem family calls their ambitious project to market wine in cultural, historic yet contemporary surroundings, is one of the exceptions.

The family's famous wine estate in the old town centre of Ober-Ingelheim has held a significant market position since the beginning of the 20th century, particularly with its popular red wines. When it became an urgent necessity to expand the areas for wine production and customer service, the estate's proprietors – by 2009, the third generation of the Wasem family – decided to acquire the former abbey nearby. The listed site dates back to the 13th century and, after an eventful history, was in need of complete renovation. In order to approach the standard required for the promising future image of the estate they envisaged, three years of building work were required to dismantle and reconstruct the abbey's basic, historic structure, including the erection of a new wing in a modern style optimised for the presentation and sale of wine. As well as a wine shop and a tasting area, the establishment also offers an extensive programme on site for gastronomic and other kinds of events. The project, in which the state heritage authorities were intensively involved, encompassed many intricate measures to renovate and rebuild the three historic building elements – such as the walls made of quarried stone blocks, the old wooden beams and rendered plaster surfaces. The site's historic abbey wing and production building were connected with a modern "joint" structure made of concrete, steel and glass. The entire building complex is particularly impressive because of its authentic, sustainable building and design materials, and its furnishings, décor and clever lighting concept.

Section
1st floor plan
Scale 1:500

1 Entrance (new building)
2 Wine shop
3 Counter
4 Tasting room
5 Office
6 Warehouse
7 Lounge

Weingut LANZ.WEIN in Nonnenhorn (Germany)

Architects: robanus architekten, Falbenhennenstraße 5,
70180 Stuttgart, Germany, www.robanus.de
Team: Eva Robanus, Stefan Robanus
Total floor area: 100 m² (excluding wine cellar)
Completed: 2012
Wine-producing region: Württemberg,
Bavarian Bodensee area
Contact: LANZ.WEIN, Sonnenbichlstraße 8,
88149 Nonnenhorn, Germany, www.lanzwein.de

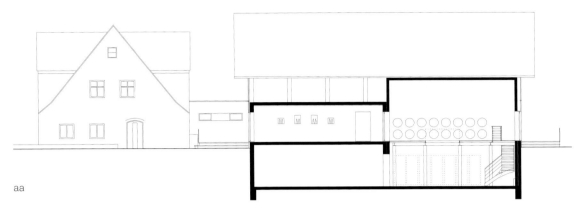

aa

Site plan   Scale 1:2000
Section   Scale 1:250

The Lanz fruit growers and wine estate in Nonnenhorn on Lake Constance has been in the family since 1836. It is currently managed by Ingeborg Lanz, her partner Johannes Haug and their son Benjamin. Organic fruit is grown on largest part of their 13.5-hectare farmland. Five years ago, the family started producing their own wine on about 2 hectares, which they sell to local restaurants and private customers. The exclusive use of mildew-resistant (in German: "PIWI", or *pilzwiderstandsfähig*) grape varieties gives the vintners their unique selling point.

The climate on Lake Constance is influenced by large amounts of precipitation – not exactly ideal conditions for producing wine. The grape varieties the Lanz family grows, however, can withstand these conditions and the types of mildew that thrive in them: *Plasmopara viticola* and powdery mildew. The directors of their wine production are Johannes Haug and young oenologist Benjamin Lanz.

In line with modern marketing, they not only redesigned the labels on the bottles, but also developed a desire to create new spaces for presenting the wine – and to integrate these spaces into the existing assets. Particularly after reorganising their wine production in 2009, the owners needed more space to develop the wine and an attractive sales

point on site. So they were looking for a minimal solution within their existing buildings.

Haug and architect Stefan Robanus have known each other from their schooldays. So it seemed appropriate to entrust this task to him. As it was very important to the family to create something that fit perfectly with the philosophy of their wine estate, they all worked together on every aspect of the planning and renovation process. The owners themselves were even physically involved in much of the renovation work.

The existing residential and office buildings were connected with a low-rise structure that was deliberately kept plain, and which contains the lavatories and an office. In the commercial building there are now areas for tasting, storing and making wine. At the same time, they reorganised and optimised the fruit storage, and some of the work rooms associated with it are new. The original character of the business building was not to be changed; however, the new sales area it contained should be more visible from the street. The external part of the building was given a smart, fresh look with a new shell made of three-layer wood panels of the same height as the connecting building. They covered the panels with an emulsion of pigments and linseed oil they mixed themselves. Depending on the direction of the light source, it almost gives them the impres-

Floor plan
Scale 1:500

1 Entrance
2 Office
3 Tasting room
4 Bottle storage
5 Wine cellar

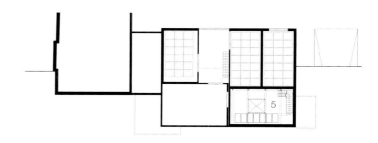

sion of having a metallic surface. The accessible area was enhanced with new plaster and wooden veneer. The planners also consciously avoided external lighting. Only the light emanating through the large shop window to the street should entice passers-by to enter and, at the same time, give them a peek into the new sales area.

The eye-catching centrepiece of the interior is the rammed-earth wall. It was layered with various kinds of clay from their own vineyard and applied over an existing brick wall. As with any idiosyncratic work of art, creating it took a great deal of patience. They built the casing for the wall themselves. After five people spent two days pounding the clay, the wall threatened to fall apart during drying. It took everyone's help to support and ultimately preserve it.
The result is impressive. The various colours and structures of the different layers of earth and the cracks that developed during the drying process make a lively impression and import a sense of the terroir into the tasting area. It gives the impression of standing in front of a cross-section of the vineyard terroir. The rectangles that they left out of the casing now serve as display windows for the wine.

An LED lamp set into the floor in front of the wall makes it stand out in relief. The result is a visualisation of growing grapes in a vineyard. The interior design is deliberately kept simple. There is a wooden table surrounded by leather-upholstered chairs in the middle of the room. The entire room oozes authenticity. It is simple, modern yet down-to-earth.

Robanus's favourite wine is Pinotin. Cabertin 2011 was designated one of the most excellent wines at a "Best of Bio 2013" tasting. The wines made from the grape varieties Johanniter, Solaris, Cabernet Blanc, Pinotin and Caberin can also be tasted and purchased here. The new sales area is additionally available for events.
The relaunch took place during the vintner festival Komm + See 2012. Many of the wine aficionados in attendance were delighted with the Lanz wines and the new premises. Since then, the tasting room has provoked much interest in people passing by. It was worth the effort. More clientele comes in – including many young people, which makes the family, which invested its heart and soul in the production of the individual yet forthright wines, very happy.

wineBANK, Weingut Balthasar Ress in Eltville-Hattenheim (Germany)

Architects: smp Generalplaner Ingenieure Sachverständige, Maximilianshof, Rheinallee 4 65346 Eltville-Erbach, Germany, www.smp-generalplaner.de
Total floor area: 300 m²
Completed: 2009
Contact: Balthasar Ress wineBANK, Hauptstraße 7, 65347 Eltville-Hattenheim , Germany, www.winebank.de

Site plan
Scale 1:800

Among the diverse possibilities that lead to a symbiosis of wine and space, the storage of wine filled into and aged in bottles within a suitable environment is probably the most natural, attractive and economically interesting option. Up to now there have been largely two alternatives for storing bottles of wine: either in the cellar of the producer or in the home of the consumer, with a good deal of technical and logistic support. Since 2009, however, there is a combination of both these storage possibilities that is as ingenious as it is simple: storing privately-owned bottles in a professional cellar. In other words, storage in optimum conditions – a constant temperature, humidity and lighting that are suitable for wine.

The idea initially sounds quite simple, but through a creative process, including planning and realisation, it developed into a complex entity that can be described as a success in concept, craft and design. This is partly due to the originator of the idea, the Rheingau vintner Christian Ress, one of

the most talented wine entrepreneurs and market-ers in the sector. After he took over responsibility of the internationally renowned VDP Balthasar Ress wine estate from his father – becoming the fifth generation to do so – he created a stir with various ventures, such as establishing a 3,000-m² vineyard on the island of Sylt, or filling Riesling into glass tubes.

The wineBANK, perhaps his most spectacular pro-ject to date, dovetails with the changing history of use of the historic Ress wine estate building. Because of a new building not far from the Rhine for wine production and storage, which features a wine tasting area, wine bar and wine shop, the old wing became obsolete in its original function. Instead, five traditional and dignified event spaces were installed in the manor house, which received a notable enhancement with the installation of the wineBANK in the vaulted cellars dating back to the 17th century and 1922.

Complicated underground work preceded the actual building which, not least because of equip-ment installation in the two-storey cellar, proved to be quite difficult. Architecturally and structurally, the project was a challenge, as it had to remain an inte-gral, recognisable part of the old vaulted cellar and profit from its climactic advantages. At the same time, the required features for a building with public access – such as emergency exits, fireproofing and lavatory facilities, which vary depending on the number of visitors – needed to be included and adequately controlled, for example with ventilation. Because of the relatively high humidity (between 65 and 90 per cent), the wine vaults are made of pumice stone panels that can adjust to a typically damp cellar climate. For the same reason, any steel elements used underwent hot-dip galvanisa-tion and powder coating to protect against rust. Authentic materials such as panels made of Bacha-rach slate for the floors and Taunus quartz added a special touch to the 300-m2 wineBANK space.

Since its completion, the wineBANK offers wine collectors and aficionados storage space within its 223 vaults of varying sizes – from 35 to 332-bottle capacity – as well as space for up to 5,500 bottles in three separate, walk-in wine cellars. This is why accessibility and security – in the form of vault-like lockers to protect against theft – were of parallel importance to the design. Using a chip card, the wineBANK can be entered at any time.
Its special flair, with colour-accented design and additional provision of wine glasses and accesso-ries at a wine bar, emphasise the service character of this establishment, which is available to its rent-ers and their guests for wine tasting. The colour scheme and LED lighting appropriate to wine add a visually striking touch, contributing to the success-ful, attractive ambience of this refuge. Finally, the modern design of the entrance to the wineBANK in the courtyard offers a striking counterpart to the original, traditional estate building, which was also restored and dates from the 19th century.

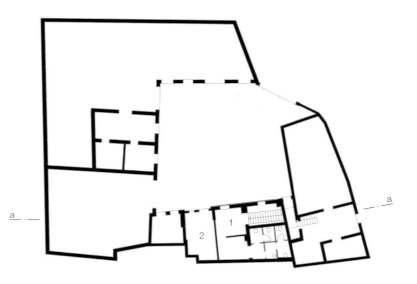

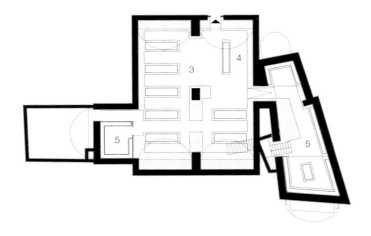

aa

Floor plan
Section
Scale 1:400

1 Entrance hall
2 Technical
  equipment
3 Vaults
4 Bar
5 Wine cellar

73

BECKER'S Weinbar in Trier (Germany)

Architects: Stein Hemmes Wirtz, Bahnhofstraße 11,
54317 Kasel, Germany, www.stein-hemmes-wirtz.de
Team: Ingbert Schilz, Jutta Schilz, Alexandra Schmitt
Total floor area: 98.92 m² (wine bar), 86.96 m² (restaurant)
Completed: 2008
Contact: BECKER'S Hotel and Restaurant,
Olewiger Straße 206, 54295 Trier, Germany,
www.beckers-trier.de

Wolfgang Becker had already been attracting attention since the 1990s with his Michelin-starred cuisine in his parents' traditional wine house, which has been in the family for five generations. Even then, he wanted to create a place that lived up to his high-quality cooking skills and embedded his culinary creations "in a modern, unique ambience". In the middle of Olewig, a part of Trier that has a village feel, the architects Hans-Jürgen Stein and Ingbert Schilz set a deliberately urban tone with their narrow, four-storey building next to Becker's parent's family restaurant. The walls of the new Michelin-starred restaurant on the ground floor are all glass. In contrast, the facade of the upper floors – where the hotel rooms are – were completely covered with basalt slabs of various colours and surfaces that come from several quarries in the Eifel region. In this way, an "a great diversity" could develop from a "parity of the materials", as the architects emphasise.

The clear minimalism of the exterior is continued inside. A wall covered with rectangular black, grey and white metal panels – inspired by the works of Wassily Kandinsky – greets the incoming guests in the entrance lounge. The basalt chosen for the flooring radiates strength and tranquillity.

Right next to the entrance there is a fully glazed wine bar with an interior that is elegant and minimalist without feeling aloof. Wood and glass are the dominant materials used here.

The main attraction, however, is behind the bar: Becker's restaurant, which was awarded two Michelin stars. The walls here are covered with basalt blocks of various sizes and surface qualities that have been set into the wall in various thicknesses, thereby creating a sense of vitality.

The kitchen is hidden behind a wall of raw oak wood. The hallway there is covered with white marble. The architects Stein and Schilz were able to transfer the uncompromising originality that makes Becker's cuisine so special into the interior design of his space. This exceptional venue's outstanding "creativity and quality" is echoed in its modern, unusually designed ambience, as described by the Gault Millau restaurant guide. It was important to Becker to create something inimitable – something that would be remembered. The great satisfaction of his guests can attest to his success.

Floor plan
Scale 1:500

1 Entrance
2 Reception
3 Lounge
4 Hotel area
5 Wine storage
6 Kitchen
7 Deliveries
8 Restaurant
9 Wine bar

La Bohème entre amis in Porto (Portugal)

Architects: AVA Architects – Atelier Veloso Architects,
Rua Formosa 168, 4000–247 Porto, Portugal,
www.ava-architects.com
Team: Carlos Jorge Coelho Veloso, Rui Filipe Coelho Veloso
Total floor area: 165 m²
Completed: 2011
Contact: La Bohème entre amis, Rua das Galerias de
Paris 40, 4050–284 Porto, Portugal, www.laboheme.com.pt

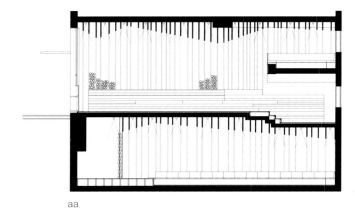

Section
Scale 1:200

aa

"Wine is the best place to meet friends." This quote is written on one of the approximately 15 chalkboards that, like a gallery, hang on the black wall behind the counter in the bar La Bohème entre amis in Porto's historic city centre. The quote comes from Brazilian author Carlos Arruda, and he could certainly have been referring to La Bohème entres amis.

Owner Alberto Fonseca, who owns a small vineyard to the north of Porto, loves wine. And he loves to enjoy it with friends, a sentiment that permeates the concept of his wine bar. When Fonseca opened Bohème – its former name – about five years ago, it was a café with an entirely different interior design. Situated in the Rua das Galerias de Paris, where one of Porto's most well-known galleries is located, the opera La Bohème was the inspiration for the café's name. Although it was financially very successful, Fonseca wanted to do something new that was more focused on wine. He therefore decided to revamp the café in the summer of 2011. He then hired Rui Veloso of AVA Architects, who had previously designed the interior of the Tendinha dos Clérigos club, which is also owned by Fonseca.

Veloso, also a lover of Portuguese wine, planned on using wood as the primary design element. Work-

ing around the idea of wine crates, the architects installed glulam made from Portuguese pine on the walls and ceiling at variable intervals of about 30 to 80 cm of the three-storey space. Inspired by the darkness in wine cellars, they chose black as the dominant colour, thereby creating a tension and contrast to the light pinewood. The flooring and all of the furniture are also made of Portuguese pine, with the bench and chair upholstery made of black synthetic leather.

During the day, the bar looks rather nondescript from the outside. But at night the interior lighting shines out into the street through the vertical wooden blinds on the facade and positively lures passing pedestrians inside. Veloso therefore managed to extend his interior design onto the exterior facade. Because of its considerably greater weather resistance, Afrimosa wood from Portugal was also used here.

During renovation, the counter was moved from the lower to the opposite, higher side of the room. At a length of 14 metres, it stretches from the entrance to the back kitchen area, thereby becoming the focal point of the bar and making Veloso successful in creating a sense of perspective for the observer that reaches deep into the room. The glulam applied to the ceiling and walls at various heights and intervals creates a lively impression full of motion. At the same time, it serves as storage area for wine behind the bar.

A gallery over the kitchen offers seating for about 20 patrons. Open at the front, it affords a generous view over the bar to the entrance. The windows on both levels looking over the back courtyard were closed and rebuilt as light boxes that provide indirect lighting. The windowless room on the lower floor has additional seating for 20 guests. Like the rest of the wine bar, the tables here have a surface area of about 40 to 60 cm and are therefore suitable for two to four people. A small raised platform serves as a stage where small concerts sometimes take place. The entire wall area behind it is a glass showcase, making it possible to display selected wines.

Generally, it was of importance to Fonseca – and this was the only stipulation he gave the architects – to display as many wine bottles as possible. An initial design, which envisaged use of the full height of the wall behind the bar as a place to present and store wines – was discarded because it would be very difficult to retrieve the bottles from that high up. Instead, the necks of the bottles are placed into opening in the vertical pine wood sections or are stored horizontally in sawed-off plastic tubes between them.

Floor plan
Scale 1:200

1 Stage
2 Lower-level seating
3 Entrance
4 Counter
5 Kitchen
6 DJ podium
7 Gallery seating

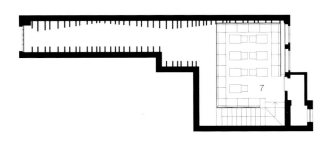

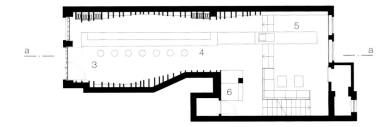

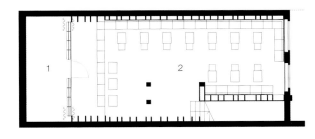

La Bohème entre amis serves only Portuguese wines. To accompany them, Fonseca offers traditional tapas and snacks. Guests can choose from about 50 wines by the bottle in addition to the 28 open bottles on offer at the bar. And although the Verdejo and Douro regions are direct neighbours of Porto, bottles from the outlying regions of Dão, Tejo and Bairrada are also represented on the wine list. The focus is solely on small, lesser-known producers, not only to support them, but also to give guests the oppor-

tunity to depart from the more well-known wines and become acquainted with new vintners.

The boards that advertise specials at the entrance and on the walls are made of a material, the mineral content of which can be tasted on the palate while drinking Castello D'Alba Branco: slate from the Douro valley. And guests can tell very quickly from the friendly service that the name La Bohème entre amis says exactly what Fonseca wanted: enjoying wine with friends.

Cata 1.81 in Barcelona (Spain)

Architects: Lagranja Design for Companies and Friends,
Pamplona 96–104, Local 12, 08018 Barcelona, Spain,
www.lagranjadesign.com
Team: José Antonio Fernández, Marta Abelló
Structural engineering: TC Projects
Total floor area: 98 m²
Completed: 2011
Contact: Cata 1.81, Calle Valencia 181, 08011 Barcelona,
Spain, www.cata181.net

The *restaurante de vinos* Cata 1.81 on Calle Valencia 181 in Barcelona's Eixample district was opened in 2011. Since then, it has become something of an insider secret in the city, far away from all the tourist traps. *La cata* – Spanish for taste or tasting – was the inspiration for the name of the restaurant, which offers its clientele a wine list of about 700 different bottles. Owner and wine lover Santi Olivella chooses his selection of mostly Spanish wines, while the five people on his kitchen team, headed by Victor Ferrer, attend to the preparation of tapas and other small, fine dishes. Inspired by international cuisine, these pioneers of modern tapas focus on local, traditional elements, which makes for an authentic and lively atmosphere every evening. Along with the enormous choice of wines by the bottle, there are also 25 excellent wines that can be ordered by the glass. Guests who are overwhelmed by the extensive range can ask for advice from a member of the friendly staff, who are very glad to give oenological guidance.

In 2011 Olivella decided to renovate his tube-shaped space, which was just barely 100 m² in size. In order to underscore the atomosphere of a small, private wine cellar, he wanted the space to receive a warm, cosy new look without losing its contemporary feel. Olivella engaged the local firm Lagranja Design to handle the makeover. The first thing they did was to bare the original walls and ceiling, and the brick, raw plaster and cement surfaces were whitewashed. The height at the entrance, which the renovation work almost doubled, was used for a new bar. It was made of

wood painted dark brown, with the countertop made of light marble. For the floor of the bar, they used recycled rubber, and the designers had pine flooring laid in the restaurant, which was left in a natural state or painted wine red. The benches along the wall were made of the same wood. In this area, narrower skirting boards of various colours were used.

All of the tables and chairs in Cata 1.81 are completely different and were especially designed for the venue by Lagranja Design. Other interior furnishings create a rather playful and very private atmosphere – such as the lamps, each of which is unique. One is made of wine glasses, for example, another out of a birdcage – with two wine bottles "perched" on its bars. On the other hand, the cloakroom and the screen in front of the office are made of plywood into which wine corks have been stuffed. The designer had a continuous mirror set along the top of the walls, in front of which there are shelves holding glasses that seem to be filled with wine. This detail visually increases the size of the narrow room and creates an intriguing interplay of colour. The witty design elements made of various different materials create a sense of a planned chaos – as though the owner had just collected them like the treasures in his wine cellar.

This light, warmly lit wine bar has a modern ambience despite its cosy design, which makes it almost feel like a living room. The eyes are drawn into a constant journey of discovery across the numerous details in the room – and the glass, cork and wine-red wood create an affinity to the wine.

Floor plan
Scale 1:200

1 Bar
2 Bar area
3 Cloakroom
4 Air space
5 Tasting area
6 Bread cupboard
7 Wine cabinet
8 Kitchen
9 Storage

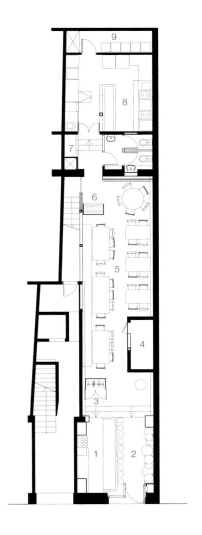

Bodega Casa Primicia in Laguardia (Spain)

Architects: Grupo Arquitelia, Calle General Urrutia 22,
26006 Logroño, Spain, www.grupoarquitelia.com
Team: Juan Marín Bueno, Javier Mateo Argómaniz
(Structural engineer)
Total floor area: 700 m²
Completed: 2008
Wine-producing region: Rioja Alavesa
Contact: Casa Primicia, Calle Páganos 78, 01300 Laguardia,
Spain, www.casaprimicia.com

The mediaeval fortress town of Laguardia lies in the Rioja Alavesa wine-producing region in the very south of the Basque territory. Bodegas (wine cellars) have existed here since the 12th century. The wine estate Casa Primicia, the cellars and wine production of which are located outside of the city, has been in the Madrid family for more than 40 years. Under the direction of Juan Ramón Madrid, classic and modern wines are produced, primarily made of the traditional Tempranillo Rioja grape variety.

The estate was named after the Casa Primicia, one of the oldest buildings in the centre of Laguardia. From the 10th to the 14th century, it was in the private ownership of various regional lords, and from the 15th to the early 19th century, it belonged to the Church. At that time, farmers here had to pay out the first and 10th part of their harvest as tax – which is how the building, which means "house of the first", got its name. It has been privately owned since it was auctioned off in 1836 and was used in various ways – until Madrid's father Julián Madrid bought it in 1972. The abandoned house was then in a decrepit state. The mediaeval stone and wood structure had defied the elements for 500 years, but the grand, wooden front gate was decayed, and the plots carved into the rock in the ground had not been used for a long time. Concrete fermentation tanks that had been built into the historic cellar in the 1960s were still in use into the 1980s. In 2006, the family decided to renovate the building entirely – with the intention of conserving its inestimable historic value. While the building was being given a new lease of life with the careful deployment of up-to-date materials, the family was also developing a fresh corporate image. The new labels and crates for wine echo a sense of the historic building: the restored wooden front gate now appears in their company logo.

Architects Juan Marín Bueno and Javier Mateo Argómaniz work for the practice Grupo Arquitelia in Laguardia. They have been friends of the wine estate for a long time, as their families supply it with grapes. Because of their existing connections to the wine producers, they were entrusted with the renovation. As they were well acquainted with the old building at Calle Páganos 78, they quickly developed a clear idea of how they would re-establish its former glory while also creating new spaces within and functions for it. In the three years that followed, the architects met weekly with the owners to act on their ideas. The main source of inspiration was the history of the area that spanned centuries, the spirit of which was to be accessible to visitors. At the same time they also wanted to be able to achieve a contemporary standard of quality. The building was renovated and rebuilt using only sandstone, oak wood and regional ceramics, augmented with steel and glass.

The large, double-leaf entrance gate was refurbished with solid oak panels according to its mediaeval archetype. When you go through it, you enter the actual wine shop – an impressive, high-ceilinged room where the wine displayed to great effect in minimalistic wooden racks can be tasted and purchased. The sandstone-brick walls, the supporting structure of sandstone blocks and the solid wood roof beams were renewed, and a new wooden, mediaeval ceiling was installed. But the wood and rammed earth floor was unable to be renovated and subsequently largely replaced with stone. The floor over the former wine storage area on the lower level, however, is made of a traversable, glazed steel construction so that you can look down into the cellar from the wine shop. Lamps were also mounted on it in order to illuminate the ground floor from below.

On the first floor, new rooms were added out of the original materials of sandstone and oak wood. These include a large meeting and tasting room that can also be used to host events. Next to this there is a large, light guest room for customers and friends of the wine estate. A sandstone staircase with sleek steel and glass landings connects the different levels.

From the ground floor, you can access the walk-in wine tanks, which were carved into the rock, by way of a steel staircase. From here, a narrow corridor leads into the vaulted cellar, which provides an optimum climate for wine storage. Not only bottles and wine barrels of different quality standards but also 201 barriques filled with "Vino de Cofradía" are stored here. This 100 per cent Tempranillo reserva wine is only produced in the very best vintage years from plots with 80-year-old vines that deliver a very low yield. It ages for 18 months in these wooden barrels before being filled into exactly 264 bottles.

1   Bodega
2   Meeting and event room
3   Guest room
4   Glass floor over the main tunnel
5   Glass floor over the historic pit and tanks
6   Display/sales
7   Historic side tunnel/barrel storage
8   Historic main tunnel/barrel and bottle storage

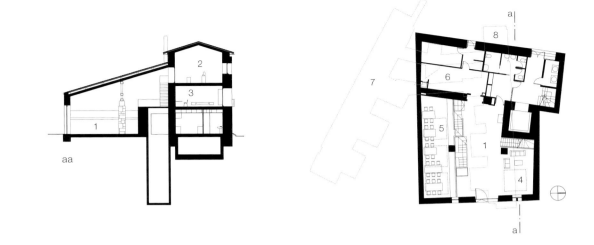

It is possible to purchase such a barrel. The *cofrade* – the buyer – can expect a few advantages. For example, his bottles are marked with a personal label. Twenty-four bottles of his barrique will be stored in a private compartment to which only he receives a key. Additionally, he may use the space for parties and spend the night in the guest room. And he will receive a 15 per cent discount on the entire wine range.

The ideal renovation of the old space and the skilful use of new elements create an atmosphere that relates the history of wine in Rioja – which is, alongside respectful treatment of nature, a central concern for the Madrid family. At the same time, Casa Primicia offers contemporary marketing opportunities. The high quality and classic style of the wines are given a fitting display here. In this noble but simple environment, surrounded by the mediaeval scenery of Laguardia, visitors can submerge themselves in the history of wine. Luxury features were deliberately left out.

When the estate was relaunched in 2009, there were several open days for the townspeople of Laguardia and local residents. The bodega is open by appointment to everyone interested in wine, history and architecture. Since the renovation and reopening of the new marketing area, there are increasing numbers of people – wine lovers in particular – who find their way to Casa Primicia. And in the future, the family are planning to host an annual gastronomic festival featuring chefs from the region.

Fiesta del Vino in Poznań (Poland)

Architects: mode:lina architekci, ulica Tatrzańska 24/2,
60-413 Poznań, Poland, www.modelina-architekci.com
Team: Jerzy Woźniak (partner), Paweł Garus (partner),
Kinga Kin, Agnieszka Owsiany
Total floor area: 120 m²
Completed: 2012
Contact: Fiesta del Vino, Ulica Czechosłowacka 106a,
61-476 Poznań, Poland, www.fiestadelvino.pl

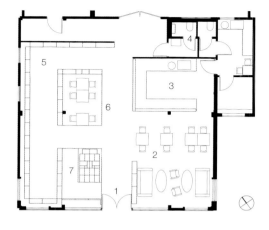

The first time they met with the architect, Jacek Walicki and his wife Dagmara still weren't sure if they wanted to make their dreams come true with a wine shop or a restaurant. They previously worked in the pharmaceutical industry but, being both enthusiastic about wine, they definitely wanted to make a switch and become their own boss with a new concept of their own. The small building that belonged to Dagmara Walicki's father used to contain a tile shop but had been empty for some time. It stood on a busy street at the edge of a residential area in south Poznań. They became acquainted with the mode:lina architectural firm through a personal recommendation. For the two young architects Jerzy Woźniak and Paweł Garus, it was their first wine-related project. Nevertheless, the owners immediately took to their presentation of two different plans. The design they preferred divided the total area of about 120 m² into different zones that could accommodate the functions of both a wine shop and a small restaurant.

The only stipulation that the Walickis made was that it should be a "very inexpensive renovation". The two architects therefore utilised simple materials. The wine racks were made out of inexpensive pine by a local carpenter. A total of 300 wines, organised by origin, stand on display here. The accompanying bottles for purchase lie horizontally

Floor plan
Scale 1:400

1 Tasting area
2 Storage/laboratory
3 Production

4 Equipment area
5 Private wine shop
6 Barrique cellar
7 Tank room
8 Warehouse

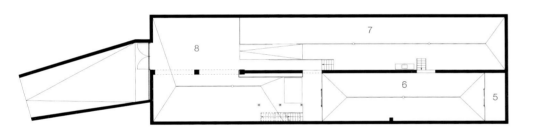

slab across the entire length of the cases on which the display wines were named. Underneath they stacked wine crates on palettes, which facilitates instant sales and quick consignments. It all makes a tranquil and orderly impression. The wine is very much the focal point of it all.

A white-stained pine bench runs around the corner and makes the room feel cosy. But the design element that makes the greatest impact is the floor. Pine floorboards varnished white run down the length of the space and give it an old-fashioned air. They came from an historic building in Vienna and

are getting a new lease of life in this building. The existing wooden ceiling and cupboard were also painted white in order to assimilated them into the general ambience. Two rows of back lamps hang from the ceiling and give the room an additional sense of spatial order. The tables were created by a local carpenter; the chairs in white and brown as well as the red cushions on the benches are from a discount furniture shop – the only dabs of colour in the otherwise restrained light of this space. It seems surprising that 46 people can be served here. But this serves to emphasise the very well

conceived, flexible design. The owners directed almost everything here themselves, while Halbritter was in charge of the construction.
To unify the outward impression, irregular form-work made of aged pine boards was placed around a large part of the facade.

The renovations were completed in 2009 and, looking back, the owners wouldn't change a thing. The family are very close and dear friends with Halbritter, who also designed Eva Koppitsch's family home on the neighbouring property.

Wine Archive at the Hotel Blaue Gans in Salzburg (Austria)

Architects: cp architektur, Christian Prasser, Nestroy-platz 1/1, 1020 Vienna, Austria, www.cp-architektur.com
Team: Wolfgang Czihak (project manager), Aniko Imrek
Total floor area: 92 m²
Completed: 2012
Contact: arthotel Blaue Gans, Getreidegasse 43, 5020 Salzburg, Austria, www.hotel-blaue-gans-salzburg.at

La vida es una gran cerdada – "Life is a bitch" is the title of the 4 × 2-metre pencil sketch by Austrian artists Peter Hauenschild and Georg Ritter, which depicts a section of a pigsty (*cerda* means "sow" in Spanish). "A work with a satirical, double meaning," says Andreas Gfrerer, the owner of Hotel Blaue Gans in Salzburg. "When I acquired it many years ago, I couldn't have known where someday the perfect place for it would be." He found that perfect place in the Wine Archive in the vaulted cellar of his hotel. The cellar, which has existed in the building since it was constructed in 1355, was used for centuries as a coal, then storage cellar. In the 1980s it was remodelled into a jazz cellar and for decades was a venue for countless concerts. Gfrerer remembers it as an element of the annual Salzburger Jazz Festival "Jazz and the City", which he co-founded. During one of the final phases of the hotel renovation, which began in 2005, a new production cellar was established in 2012 opposite what is today the Wine Archive. This was primarily for storing the necessary utilities for the building; additionally, it simplifies deliveries, which can now take place through its own entrance.

The idea not to plan a separate storage area for wine evolved during cellar renovations. Architect Christian Prasser, who had stood by Gfrerer over the previous 10 years during all phases of his hotel

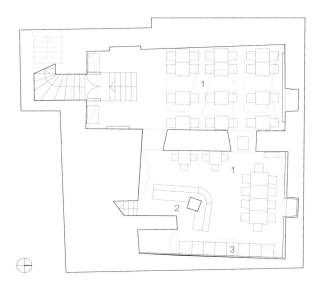

Floor plan
Scale 1:250

1 Tasting area
2 Bar
3 Wine refrigerator

renovation, suggested "combining storage and service", thereby giving guests the opportunity to "dine in the warehouse". That was how the idea emerged to present wine in the newly created Wine Archive in the former jazz cellar.

It was important for the architect to keep the existing conglomerate stone vaults visible, thereby maintaining the atmosphere of the cellar. The existing stone floor made of marble mosaic from the nearby Austrian town Adnet was kept in its original state and only augmented where necessary.

In order to avoid large interventions into the structure of the old building, lighting fixtures were integrated into a construction made of oak wood slats that was set into the vaulted ceiling. The bar area was also covered with oak wood slats, which give the surface a three-dimensional feel. The slat construction also emphasises the warehouse atmosphere of the spaces. The tables were individually welded out of steel channels embedded in rustic oak boards as tabletops. On the whole, the materials were deliberately limited to steel and oak wood, which emphasise the simple charm of the vaulted cellar.

The wine refrigerator has a capacity of almost 1,500 bottles. Its front and sides are all glass, but it was left open at the back in order to avoid reflections as well as display the bottles stored in it in front of the historic stone wall. To prevent conden-sation, a general ambient zone of about 16–17°C for both white and red wines was created. This puts red wine at its proper drinking temperature; white wine is cooled to the necessary 8–12°C before serving. Using indirect lighting in the doors of the wine cupboard, attention is drawn to the bottles within it without any adverse effect to the mystical atmosphere of the room. At the same time, it makes the labels easily legible.

In the middle of both rooms there is an old Berkel meat slicer, on which special ham delicacies from Lungau, Styria or northern Italy are displayed – sliced paper thin and served with homemade dishes from the hotel's own food kitchens, and garnished with herbs from its own herb garden. To accompany this, guests can choose an appropriate wine themselves from the wine cabinet. The Wine Archive can accommodate about 60 people.

The Blaue Gans is a kind of refuge in the middle of Salzburg. Its guests should feel comfortable in this art hotel and its natural yet modern-looking rooms, art displays, restaurant, brasserie, guests' garden and library. The owner and architect were successful in augmenting the hotel with the further attraction of the Wine Archive. It's more than just a wine cellar – it's a concept for the palate and senses.

Weingut Neumeister in Straden (Austria)

Architect: Andreas Burghardt, Mariahilfer Straße 105,
1060 Vienna, Austria, www.burghardt.co.at
Total floor area sales/tasting: 2,500 m²
Completed: 2006
Wine-producing region: Styria
Contact: Weingut Neumeister, Straden 42
A–8345 Straden, www.neumeister.cc

The labels on the bottles of wine from the Neumeister wine estate in Straden, in the south-eastern part of Styria, are sleek and timeless. The fact that it was Andreas Burghardt who designed them following his successful expansion of the estate bears witness to the high level of trust and common understanding between client and architect. Having designed the interior of the new building added to the winery at the end of the 1990s, his services were again called upon when it came time to add another extension in 2004, this time by Christoph Neumeister and his brother Matthias. At the time, they were assuming increasing responsibility for the wine estate and designing the already completed shell construction. The clients wanted bring about a clear segregation between the different groups of

visitors. While conference guests would continue to be received in the existing, older building complex, they favoured the creation of premises for groups and business partners that could be separated, thus ensuring a parallel, problem-free flow of visitors. They also wanted to enable unhindered access to the winery for older and physically disabled people – from the entrance area at street level right down to the cellar and all the levels in between. The owners also wanted to provide their customers with a convenient means of picking up their wine.

The wine estate is barely discernible to arriving visitors, which is in keeping with the owners' philosophy. To them, it is not about showing how big the now 30-hectare wine estate, known far beyond the southeastern part of Styria, is to the outside world. Ivy climbs up steel cables which, in turn, are attached to a steel framework that gives the appearance of being superimposed onto the building. It is only a question of time until what is still visible of the white concrete walls is completely covered by the evergreen screen. A sign with the words *"Weinverkauf"* (wine for sale) guides visitors to a tall, simple entrance door. Once inside, the visitor's gaze falls on the floor-to-ceiling glass wall opposite, which is already almost completely hidden by the ivy hanging down outside. The three large, apricot-coloured pendant lights that hang in front of it contrast with the light green of the ivy –

especially when the sun is shining. The lights, which can also be found in the lower-level tasting area, were custom-made according to a design created by Burghardt. The stairs leading down to the lower level are elm clad, and the fine structure of the wood gives them an elegant yet unobtrusive appearance. The stairs take visitors to the bright and open tasting area, which has a large floor-to-ceiling glass wall that offers a view of the outside terrace. The ceiling, walls and columns, all made from fair-faced concrete, contrast with the oak parquet flooring and the elm wood panelling. A conscious decision was made to forgo a bar counter; instead the wines can be tasted by several guests at the same time at the long bar table, also made of elm and designed by Burghardt. A small niche integrated to one side under the stairs and made from the same wood provides a place to sit.

From here, the view upwards stretches all the way to the top floor. A rack for displaying wine and books stands beside it, next to the stairs. On the other side is a large tasting room, which can be closed off by a sliding door. The walls, filled with empty wine bottles stacked in 10 layers, one on top of the other, right up to the ceiling, are an impressive sight. In an open spiral formation, the installation spans the entire the room, dividing it into a smaller front section and a larger rear section. It was very important to the architect that he find

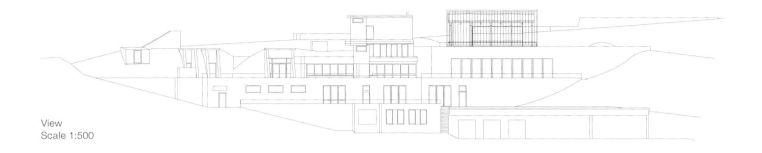

View
Scale 1:500

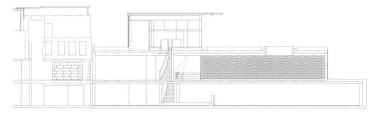

aa

bottles in exactly the right colour: on the one hand, the "wall of bottles" should let in enough light to allow the overall size of the room to register, at the same time he wanted the wall to act as a visual barrier separating the rooms. He succeeded in managing this balancing act most impressively by selecting an antique green. Here again, it is the pendant light fixtures that serve as a strong design element, contrasting with the fair-faced concrete ceiling and the oak parquet floor. Two tables designed by Burghardt and built by his Viennese carpenter Helmut Klar in the rear section of the room and one table in the front section can each accommodate approximately 10 people. As chairs, Burghardt selected a classic from the 1950s: the stacking chairs designed by the architect Roland Rainer for Vienna City Hall, which are again being manufactured today.

A lift connects the different floors and makes it easy to transport crates of wine from the stockroom to the upper levels. The wine shop is located adjacent to the tasting room. Rare wines, stored at just the right temperature, can be seen through the floor-to-ceiling glass wall that serves as a visual link between the wine shop and the tasting room. Anybody listening to Christoph Neumeister's descriptions quickly realises just how strongly he identifies with the architecture here. Burghardt, who subsequently remodelled the gourmet restaurant – Saziani Stub'n, also part of the building – as well as the local Greißlerei, a sales outlet for regional products located in the middle of the town – has succeeded in creating a timeless and sophisticated piece of architecture in Straden which, as Christian Neumeister puts it, "will still be nice to look at in 20 years".

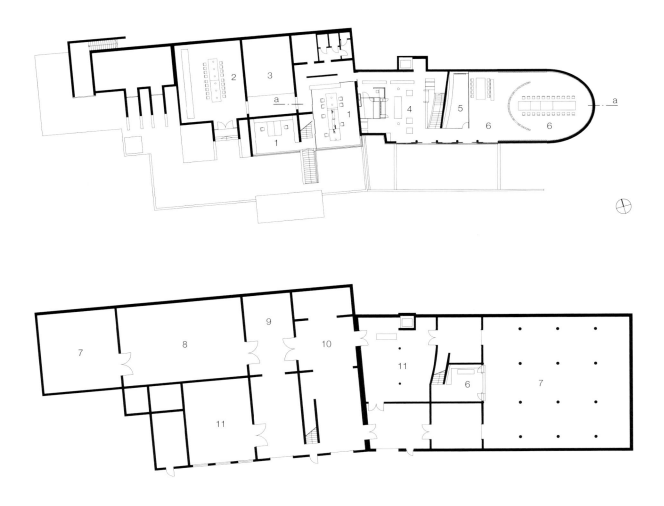

GRAPY.SHOP in Roosendaal
(the Netherlands)

Architects: Storeage, Overtoom 197-4,
1054 HT Amsterdam, the Netherlands, www.store-age.nl
Team: Leendert Tange (creative director),
Joao Carneiro (3D designer), Sarah Napier (2D designer)
Completed: 2011
Contact: GRAPY.SHOP, Passage Roosendaaal, Passage 1,
4701 AN Roosendaal, the Netherlands, www.grapy.nl

That books and wine can successfully form a symbiotic relationship is not solely demonstrated by the publication of this new volume. The reading of an exciting novel can be accompanied only too gladly by a glass of good wine; the mouth-watering recipes in a cookbook whet the palate for a fine wine to accompany the food.

The renowned and well-stocked Amsterdam-based online wine retailer Grapy.nl carries a selection of approximately 3,000 wines. A special feature of the website is WineStein, an "online sommelier", which makes it easy for customers to find a wine to complement a meal. All they have to do is enter the main ingredients, additional components and how the dish is being prepared to get suggestions for wine pairings.

In 2011, Grapy.nl decided to translate this idea into a small bricks-and-mortar store and found a partner in the Roosendaal bookstore Het verboden rijk, where approximately 70 wines are displayed on 25 m² of space. Some of the wines and books are displayed next to each other, which can lead to interesting encounters.

The wines can of course be bought at the store, a transaction that often goes hand-in-hand with the purchase of a book; larger quantities of wine from the extensive selection can be ordered online and delivered to one's home. WineStein is also available as an app, providing any help needed "on-site" – should the perusal of an inspiring cookbook lead to the desire to take the right wines home at the same time.

The Amsterdam-based retail design agency Storeage, which boasts many years of experience with store design and the presentation of goods, was commissioned to the create the "shop in a shop". Grapy.nl tasked Storeage with designing and executing the entire project. The GRAPY.SHOP is intended to make the wines more accessible – an online shop can never match the advice and personal touch provided by a conventional store.

The wine bottles are displayed in stackable, interlocking wooden units which also serve as storage space. This modular system makes the display easy to reorganise or rearrange. The wooden units are painted in muted colours that symbolise the different varieties of wine. They vary from yellow-green (light, fresh and fruity white wine) to aubergine (full-bodied, dense red wine). As it is easy to write in chalk on the matte surface of the units, information such as wine type, characteristic flavour, price or suggested food pairings can be written directly on

A modular system of stackable display units, examples of colour combinations that mimic the colour scheme in the WineStein app:
a "Powerful Whites"
b "Sweets"
c "Powerful Red"

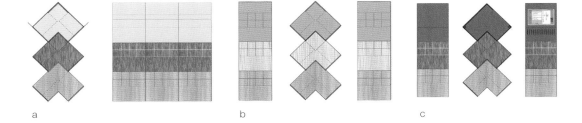

a   b   c

the wine displays. The colour scheme matches the one used in the WineStein app, which makes it easier to further narrow down the wine selection. The walls – covered with decorative illustrations of fish, vegetables and pasta – are also painted in subdued colours, thus playing their part in creating a warm and inviting ambience.

The online sommelier – in the form of a column with an interactive touchscreen – is available for consultation in the middle of the store. This is where customers can get quick and easy suggestions for the best wine pairing or place orders with Grapy.nl. The relaxed approach to wine does away with any fears or reservations, allowing even those who do not know that much about wine to find the right wine to suit their particular occasion.

Customers from the surrounding area love to visit the store with its eye-catching design – simply to browse the books or peruse the selection of wines. Het verboden rijk and GRAPY.SHOP share the same shop front and use it for cross-marketing sales promotions. Thanks to this strategy, customer traffic has doubled since 2011.

Beros & van Schaik Wine Traders in Bucharest (Romania)

Architects: Beros & Abdul Architects, Strada Smardan 9,
030071 Bucharest, Romania, www.sod.ro
Team: Christian Beros, Esenghiul Abdul, Claudia Trufas
Total floor area: 50 m²
Completed: 2012
Contact: Beros & van Schaik Wine Traders Strada Covaci 19,
033071 Bucharest, Romania, www.bvswines.ro

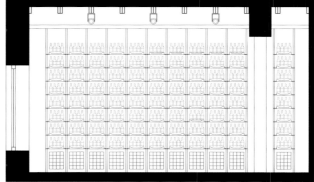

Sections
Scale 1:100   aa

The 2010 Castillo de Molina Carmenère in the wine rack of the small wine shop Beros & van Schaik Wine Traders in Bucharest comes from a long way away. As does Christian Beros, one of the two owners of BvS Wine Traders. Raised in Santiago de Chile, he came to Bucharest on business after completing his degree in architecture in Chile and spending several years in London. In addition to running his own firm of architects, he exploited his private contacts to Chilean winemakers and began importing their wines to Romania. He met a wine-loving partner, who was already operating a successful hotel in Bucharest, in the person of Jerry van Schaik. Together, they expanded the existing import business to include wines from Spain, France, Italy, New Zealand and Australia. They founded BvS Wine Traders, which not only imports the wines but also markets them to hotels, restaurants and bars. Initially, all the wines were imported, but the selection of wines changed as contacts with native Romanian winemakers widened. Today, almost two-thirds of the wines that BvS Wine Traders carries are Romanian.

With the decision to open a shop and wine bar in 2012, Beros and van Schaik wanted to increase focus on the end customer in combination with their web shop. This would give guests the opportunity to taste the wines before purchasing them.

The premises are ideally situated in the centre of Bucharest. Beros, who designed the interior of the bar, removed the existing suspended ceiling, thus exposing the full height of walls, which he uses to display the wines. Reminiscent of a library, shelves stretch from the floor to the ceiling, which has been left in its unfinished state. The wines are presented on veneer plywood shelves, which are fastened to iron supports using metal clamps and thus resemble scaffolding. A long wall counter with integrated showcases for presenting special wines is mounted on the opposite wall. The wines available by the glass, which change weekly, are written on boards hanging above the counter. The wall below the counter is tiled with white tiles.

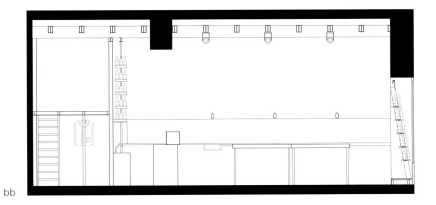

bb

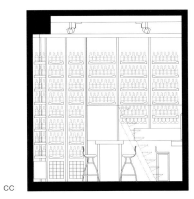

cc

Floor plan
Scale 1:100

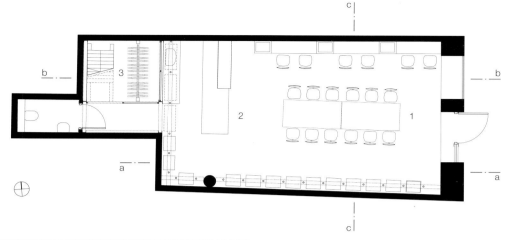

Contrary to the usual practice in Romania of sitting at individual tables, Beros placed a large, long table with a top made of rustic oak planks in the middle of the room. Bar stools, fashioned from wood and iron, were made to match. The floor is made of unfinished, fair-faced concrete. The back of the store has been divided using a metal lattice to create a small storeroom and office space. A counter created from poured concrete stands in front of it, an enclosure made of veneer plywood screens the cash desk.

The use of materials that have primarily been left in their raw state gives the fittings an "industrial character", as Beros puts it, ensuring that focus remains on the wine. It was also important to the architect that the wine is presented in a bright, unobtrusive environment so that guests take notice of the labels and bottles.

Large, black light fixtures are installed on the ceiling and illuminate the wall and shelves from the

side. Industrial light fittings, which Beros acquired in London, hang from the ceiling in between, bathing the room in warm light.

Every Thursday evening, a different selection of wines is presented, often in the presence of the winemakers. Five different wines can be tasted, accompanied by a brief presentation. The wines are accompanied by cheese, bread and cured ham – food traditionally served with wine. The wine bar is busy on weekends. There is, as Beros says, a kind of "BvS-Community" who all know each other. In addition to enjoying fine wines, professional and private contacts are established. This is also how several of his commissions for architectural projects have come about. The wine bar is, for both owners, "like a puzzle", where one thing leads to another: entertainment, contacts and enjoyment. Beros would someday like to have a wine from his own vineyard on the shelves. He does not yet know what it will be called – but there is still plenty of time to decide.

eTT? in Bruneck (Italy)

Architect: Walter Angonese, Marktplatz 6, 39052 Kaltern,
Italy, www.angonesewalter.it
Artistic assistant: Manfred Alois Mayr, 39100 Bolzano, Italy
Collaborator: Theodor Gallmetzer, 39100, Bolzano, Italy
Total floor area: 35 m²
Completed: 2006
Contact: Bar eTT?, Gilmplatz 1/a, 39031 Bruneck, Italy

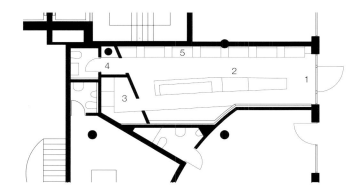

Floor plan
Scale 1:200

1 Entrance
2 Bar
3 Service area
4 Restrooms
5 Bench

"Et?" – this expression in the dialect spoken in the Puster Valley could often be heard when Hildegard Stabinger and Walter Angonese were working together with craftsman on remodelling the bar on Gilmplatz in Bruneck, South Tyrol. *Et* can best be translated by the expression "right?" or "don't you think?" added to the end of a sentence. The new bar was named after this little word, which is conducive to diplomatic communication. To avoid confusion with the Hollywood movie *ET*, an additional "T" was added.

Stabinger, owner of the eTT? bar, worked for a long time as maitre d' of the restaurant gretl am see on Lake Kaltern. The desire to create something of her own and a longing to return to her native Puster Valley led to the decision to lease a room on the ground floor of the Hotel Post in Bruneck. The old Hotel Post (not to be confused with the new Hotel Post) was an institution in Bruneck, as this was where well-known personalities liked to rub shoulders. It was, however, torn down in 2002 and rebuilt during the two years that followed in a style that reflected the original character of the town.

Architect Angonese had been a frequent guest of Stabinger's at gretl am see. One day she surprised him with a rough draft of the design for the space. The architect's first impulse was to decline for lack of time, but then he made a few first sketches while still seated in the restaurant. Ultimately, however, he agreed to help. The challenge was to make optimal use of the long narrow room, which measured a mere 3.2 x 9 m, and refit it. The American Bar in Vienna, designed by Adolf Loos, served as inspiration. The aim was not to create a space that was "the latest contemporary craze" but rather an appealing, functional space that was inviting and cosy while at the same time anything but old fashioned. Angonese and artist Manfred Alois Mayr took up this intriguing challenge.

The floor was laid with grey sandstone slabs from Tuscany. The left half of the room is taken up by a solid oak bar, the front part of which juts into the room, allowing guests to sit on bar stools. The rear section of the bar is perfect for standing. This is where a large handrail designed by Mayr, made of turned solid wood and painted black, has been mounted. This three-dimensional element not only establishes a relationship to artisan tradition but also conveys haptic sensuality. Here the guest can linger, touch and find, support in a literal sense. The middle section of the bar has a glass-enclosed cut-out, which serves as a display case for wines and small snacks. The regional wines on offer are displayed on the shelves on the wall behind the bar. Mirrors create a greater sense of space and give the room depth. At the

rear section of the bar is a trapezoid recess that is used as both storage space and work surface.
A solid oak bench runs along the right-hand wall. The back of the bench is divided into two sections with a number of white wooden tables inserted into the groove in the middle; the tables can be pushed together as needed. This allows small groups to sit together, or all the table can be pushed together to create one long table where appetizers and finger food can be served, depending on the occasion.

The wines served by the glass and upcoming events are chalked up on a wall-mounted blackboard that runs the full length of the bench. Sprayed plaster was used on the wall above the blackboard and on the ceiling. This type of plaster, which is difficult to work with, is painted white and creates an authentic mood.
The round pendant ceiling lights made of black steel and frosted glass were designed by Angonese and Mayr. They create a pleasant, soft light. No changes were made to the facade, the entrance or the stainless steel framed glass doors.
As neon signs are prohibited in Bruneck, a little trick was used for the lettering of eTT?: the letters are made from backlit glass.

The owner is completely satisfied with the result. The dominant colour brown, combined with the white elements, gives the room a cosy yet contemporary ambiance. The narrowness of the space, of which optimal use has been made, is cosily warming in winter, and there is shaded seating outside for hot summer days.

Just six months after planning began, the bar was opened in March 2006 with a party. eTT? is open weekdays from early morning to early evening. In the morning and afternoon, students and office workers come in for a coffee or to enjoy one of the homemade snacks such as brioche and panini sandwiches. After work, it is a place where people like to meet up for an aperitif.
In addition to the wines from regional winemakers and wineries, drinks such as Sprizz and Hugo are also on offer. Stabinger considers the Prosecco Foss Marai Extra Dry to be particularly noteworthy, and one of Angonese's favourite wines is the Réserve del Conte von Manincor.

Cantina Antinori nel Chianti Classico in Bargino (Italy)

Architects: Archea Associati, Lungarno Benvenuto, Cellini 13, 50125 Florence, Italy, www.archea.it
Team: Laura Andreini, Marco Casamonti, Silvia Fabi, Giovanni Polazzi
Total floor area: 40,000 m²
Completed: 2012
Wine-producing region: Chianti
Contact: Cantina Antinori nel Chianti Classico, Via Cassia per Siena 133, Bargino, 50026 San Casciano in Val di Pesa, Italy, www.antinorichianticlassico.it

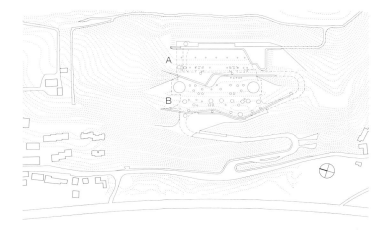

Site plan
Scale 1:7,500

After the Etruscans introduced wine production into Tuscany in the 8th century BCE, the region developed over the centuries into one of the world's top regions for quality wines. As an integral part of its history and culture, wine is still of great import here today.

The roots of the Florentine Antinori family can be traced all the way back to the 12th century. The aristocratic family has been producing wine since as early as 1385 – the year that Giovanni di Piero Antinori became a member of the Florentine Guild of Winemakers. Today, the still family-run enterprise has 14 wine estates around the world. The head office is located in the Palazzo Antinori, which was built in the 1460s. The Marchesi Antinori have been living here, in the heart of Florence, the capital city of the region of Tuscany and a city surrounded by Chianti vineyards, since 1506. The offices of the company – managed today by the 25th and 26th generations of the family, Marchese Piero Antinori and his three daughters Albiera, Allegra and Alessia – were also situated there until 2012. It was also where some of the Chianti Classico wines were produced and stored. Several years ago, it became clear that the town house was too small to keep pace with the increasing demands being made upon it. In addition to the need to build a new winery, the family also wanted to create a visitor centre where wine enthusiasts could come into direct contact with the philosophy for producing wine handed down through the family for generations. The perfect location was found in Bargino, in the middle of the Chianti Classico region between Florence and Siena. It was intended that the new wine estate not only be a place where wine was made but should also include a wine shop, restaurant and museum. The idea was to create a building that blended seamlessly – almost invisibly – with the surrounding countryside, an homage to Tuscany, full of respect for the land. With this plan in mind, the family approached the international firm of architects Archea Associati in Florence in 2005. Archea's co-founder Marco Casamonti and, acting

on behalf of the client, Albiera Antinori were placed in charge, developing the project together.

A large building complex, which descends the hillside by degrees and spans two levels, was created. By planting the roofs with vines and olive trees, the building appears to be part of the landscape, resembling terraced vineyards. This detail is intended to express deep-rooted ties with the land. Materials such as steel, concrete, terracotta, glass and oak were used, all materials that are also used in the winemaking process: steel, concrete, wood and terracotta in the form of fermentation vessels and glass bottles for bottling the wine. All these unassuming materials were supplied by manufacturers from the region.

The concrete used for the building was mixed with iron oxide to give it a reddish tinge. Corten steel was selected for the outer skin of the building, its red-brown colour serving as a reference to the earth. If the new wine estate is approached by car along the road, one runs the risk of driving right past it – that is the extent to which the expansive new building disappears into the vineyards. Its existence is revealed only by the sign "Cantina

Antinori" at the entrance and two visible rust-brown stretches of the Corten facade.

Once past the gatehouse, a long driveway leads to the underground parking level. This is where the foot of the matrix-like spiral staircase, constructed from concrete and Corten steel and leading to all three levels, can be found. This striking construction should not be viewed as merely functional but rather as a sculpture within the context of the building. It leads from its dark belly to the brightest, uppermost level, which offers a panoramic view of the countryside. Marco Casamonti asserts that it is an allusion to the spiral in Dante's Divine Comedy, which leads from hell to purgatory to paradise. As the construction of a spiral staircase is a major challenge for any architect, he is particularly proud of this detail.

The stairs lead up to the terrace in front of the entrance. From here, one not only has a wonderful view of the sweep of the elliptical staircase, which leads outside and up to the next level, but one's gaze can be allowed to wander over the countryside and the vines growing in front of the building. The lobby is entered through a glass door – on this level, the front of the almost 100 m-wide new

building is made entirely of glass. A large, round skylight is located above the stairs leading to the second floor. A lattice made of triangular terracotta struts allows in daylight while at the same time providing protection against the hot midday sun. The architects borrowed this element from traditional country homes in Tuscany. As the second level is open in the direction of the reception area, both floors profit from the pleasant, even light. The balustrade of the gallery, which also constitutes the ceiling of the lobby, is made of Corten steel. Light strips are installed in narrow, rectangular cut-outs.

Instead of solid walls, the eye is drawn to slightly inclining room dividers which also serve as shelves. The elements, which were created from segments of rectangular pipe made of grey terracotta, form a loose pattern due to the way in which they have been stacked at irregular angles, bringing movement into the space. Long light fixtures made of brass tubing hang over the large, solid oak reception desk, bathing the entire space in a warm, bright light. A glassed-in room with colourful, felt-upholstered furniture and deep-pile carpets, situated between the reception desk and corridor,

extends an enticing invitation to linger and read about wine and architecture or simply allow the mind to wander. Visitors will encounter the colourful, "sculpted" chairs again as cosy lounge elements in a number of different places.

Passing the desk on the left, visitors are first guided to the auditorium, where an extremely interesting film about the construction of the new wine estate is shown. This venue is also available for training courses, presentations and meetings. What is remarkable about this small cinema is that not only the walls but also the ceiling is constructed to resemble an irregular wood relief – an allusion to wine barrels. That is where grapes ferment to create fine wine; this is where ideas and concepts "ferment". At the same time, the wood panelling improves the acoustics. The tiered rows of seats are constructed from oak to which contour seats have been mounted; the rounded shape of the seats and their felt upholstering in varying shades of green and purple allude to the different stages of development of the grapes and vegetation in the vineyards.

The light-flooded museum is the next stop. The Antinori family is by tradition one of the leading art lovers and patron of the arts among the aristocratic families of Tuscany. Contemporary paintings, sculptures and installations can be seen here in dialogue with art from previous centuries, which – in line with the museum's concept – bear reference to the family and viniculture. The exhibits include a replica of the wine press designed by Leonardo da Vinci. Older paintings include members of the Antinori family and illustrate the course of history and the changes it has wrought. The contemporary artists Yona Friedman, Rosa Barba and Jean-Baptiste Decavèle have created works of art "in situ", meaning that they were created for the space and in the space. Friedman's monumental *Ikonostasi* about the ongoing transition in architecture, Decavèle's film that constructs a picturesque narrative of the artworks in the Palazzo Antinori and Barba's large installation in the inner courtyard.

After the visit to the museum, the tour continues in the wine cellar. On this level, a heavy iron door affords entry onto a walkway suspended at mid-height, which leads through the vaulted cellar. The room is dark and cool and dimly lit by lights set in the floor. The wine is left to mature in peace. The three seamlessly connected vaults, with their asym-

metrical sweep, are completely clad with terracotta tiles. The lattice made of triangular struts used to construct the skylight is repeated on the end walls. The shape of the vaults and the open side walls, reminiscent of church windows, give the room a somewhat sacral air. This impression is reinforced by three balconies, one of which is open and can be entered through a corridor. The two balconies opposite are enclosed by glass and form part of a conference and tasting room. They project into the room like loggias.

At the other end of the walkway is a stairwell made from the same reddish-brown concrete as the building itself. Because the joins between the rectangular elements have not been sealed, it looks like it has been constructed from sandstone blocks. The staircase made of Corten steel connects three floors and floats freely in the stairwell. The choice of colours, the impression of stone blocks and the subdued lighting almost create the feeling of being inside a pyramid. At the bottom of the stairs is a steel door; all the traces from working on the door, like the screws and seams, have deliberately been left visible. This door leads back into the vaulted barrel cellar. Standing among the countless barrique barrels, which are arranged in double rows, the true dimensions of the three-part vault are revealed. From this perspective, its curve gives the impression of a huge tent; despite its massive size, the room seems light and airy.

There is a small room at the back of the vault where the rare wines and older vintages are stored. A table made of steel with simple, wooden chairs placed around it stands in the middle. Once again, emphasis is placed on ensuring an optimal climate for the wine rather than maintaining a temperature which those tasting the fine wines here might find more comfortable. A particularly interesting detail is the ceiling, which curves down rather than up. This "vestry" reinforces the impression of being in a temple dedicated to wine.

Visitors then take the stairs up to the third floor, where the vin santo – the classic Tuscan dessert wine – is produced in small barrels, and olive oil (the wine estate is also surrounded by numerous olive groves) in large terracotta containers. The restaurant, Rinuccio 1180, named after the patriarch of the family, is also located on this level. Here one can enjoy regional, freshly prepared cuisine, which

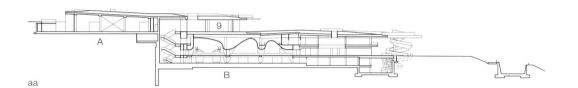

aa

A

B

9

Section · Floor plan
Scale 1:1,500

1 Terrace
2 Lobby
3 Administration
4 Shop
5 Museum
6 Auditorium
7 Tasting
8 Inner courtyard
9 Restaurant

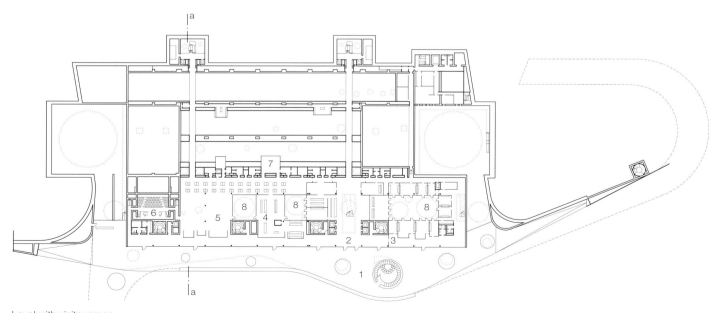

Level with visitor areas

is, of course, always paired with the appropriate Antinori wines. The panorama window – or, weather permitting, the terrace – offers a spectacular view of the broad sweep of the countryside. The tour ends in the wine shop, where familiar design elements, such as the terracotta tiles and steel, have been used here to construct the counter and showcases. All the furniture is made of Corten steel or oak. The room dividers, which already caught the eye in the lobby, give the room a light and airy feel. Exactly six bottles of wine fit in each of these irregularly shaped, four or five-cornered, terracotta showcases. In addition to a large selection of the estate's own wines, which can also be tasted here, regional culinary specialties and glass goods available for sale are also displayed in these unique showcases. The wine shop also includes a temperature-controlled, glass-enclosed room, where the particularly fine wines are stored. A bookshop has also been incorporated, which is designed in the same style as the wine shop but offers a quieter atmosphere in which one can browse at leisure. The large floor-to-ceiling windows at the front of the long building complex allow plenty of daylight to enter and offer a fascinating panoramic view of the countryside. As the glass is extra clear and non-reflecting, white circles were added later here and there to avoid accidents. Because they occur at irregular intervals, they resemble the bubbles in a sparkling wine.

Ever since the wine estate was opened in October 2012, it has been attracting increasing numbers of wine enthusiasts, tourists and architects. Because the family has a great interest in communicating their wine philosophy, tours offering numerous, detailed anecdotes and a wealth of information are available. Albiera Antinori recalls with some amusement the mixed reactions of the local population: they assumed, tongue in cheek, that the ultramodern building would not remain standing long as it was already starting to rust. She responds to scepticism like this by pointing out that the Palazzo Antinori in Florence, which was completed in 1469, was far ahead of its time. Wine and architecture have formed a symbiotic relationship in Tuscany since as early as the Renaissance – the new Cantina spans the period up to the present day.

Restaurant Löwengrube in Bolzano (Italy)

Architects: bergmeisterwolf architekten, Brunogasse 3, 39042 Bressanone, Italy, www.bergmeisterwolf.it
Total floor area: 478 m²
Completed: 2012
Contact: Restaurant Löwengrube, Zollstange 3, Piazza Dogana, 39100 Bolzano, Italy www.loewengrube.it

A red lion over a stylised Ö – together they make up the new logo of Löwengrube, a restaurant in Bolzano's historic city centre that has a long tradition dating back to 1543. From the outside, the venerable building has a historic flair, while remodelling has completely transformed the interior. After the previous tenant left, the family who own the building initially only wanted to make a few changes to the rooms on the ground floor. The plan was to open up the smaller dining area situated next to the main dining area by removing a wall, make the existing kitchen a little bit bigger, install a new bar, replace the floors and update the lavatories. The owners contacted the firm of architects bergmeisterwolf in Bressanone, which had been recommended to them, in the middle of 2010.

During the course of meetings to discuss planning with the two architects Michaela Wolf and Gerd Bergmeister, it soon became clear that the changes to the ground floor would be more extensive than originally intended. As a result of the decision to move the kitchen to the upper floor and connect it by a service lift to the dining areas, the room in the front was completely opened up, and the entrance was moved to the western side of the building. This means that guests now enter what was previously the smaller dining area – and now a lounge – through a vestibule made from raw steel. Like a cube without a fixed connection point, it appears to float above the floor and sets itself apart from the rest of the space as a separate entity. The glass fronted, walk-in wine cabinet where the white wines are stored provides a first hint of Löwengrube's extensive wine list. The lounge is where guests can sit in classic egg chairs and sip an aperitif before going into the dining area to eat.

The back wall and ceiling are constructed from tapered, untreated oak boards that have been joined using shadow joints and which also serve as soundproofing.

Cylindrical, hanging light fixtures give off a warm light. The architects left the historic tiled stove untouched – it symbolises a link between the past and present. On the back wall of the lounge, a selection of wines is offered for sale on shelves constructed from raw steel. Apart from wood, steel is the dominant material in the new Löwengrube restaurant. In its raw state, it provides a contrast to the time-honoured walls, which are steeped in history, and at the same time has the strength of character, says Bergmeister, to coexist alongside them. The ceiling lights, which provide additional lighting for the shelves and bar area, were also made from steel according to a design created by the architects. The long bar counter, positioned laterally across the open space, creates a direct line of

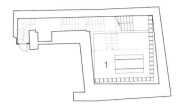

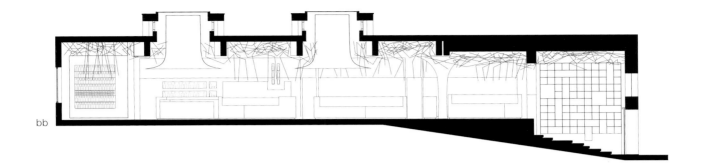

Via Silla is a bustling street in the Prati neighbour-hood, not far from the Vatican. The residential area, which evolved gradually from the end of the 18th century on, is a combination of old and new build-ings which vary in height and architectural style. Numerous traditional restaurants, bakeries, cheese shops and butcher shops are located in this pleas-ant and vibrant neighbourhood. Four award-win-ning top chefs selected what had once been an Alfa Romeo dealer's show room as the venue in which to open up a restaurant with wine bar and wine shop on approximately 400 m² of space. The premises also incorporate a bakery and sale space for regional cheese and sausage specialities. Cristina Bowerman comes from Apulia. Although the former lawyer enjoyed cooking as a child, she did not decide until later to turn her passion into a profession and first spent several years in the US. After returning to her native country, she opened her first restaurant, Glass, in 2006 in Rome together with Silvia Sacerdoti in Trastevere. By 2010, she had already been awarded a highly coveted Michelin star. At the end of 2012, she opened Romeo – a fusion of restaurant, wine bar and coffee bar – together with her partner Fabio Spada as well as Alessandro and Pier Luigi Roscioli. Sacerdoti and all four chefs are the creative minds behind the new culinary meeting point at the heart of Italy's capital.

Spada and Sacerdoti have known the architect Andrea Lupacchini for a long time – as he had designed Glass, it was a given that they would

entrust their friend with the task of remodelling and decorating Romeo. They imagined a magical, dynamic space with emotional appeal, where guests could not only enjoy Italian and international wines but first and foremost freshly prepared food. The chefs see their mission as reviving a taste for pure, authentic food. They view the globalisation of taste and the successive disappearance of trad-itional dishes as a tragedy. They would like to inspire the younger generation, in particular, with simple and healthy dishes created from top-quality ingredients. Romeo regularly offers tasting menus. Once a month, a winemaker presents his or her wines, which may then be sold directly to the guests. Which wine is best paired with which dish is decided together with one of the chefs and the guests. Set menus, snacks, wines and the regular events are deliberately offered at affordable prices – the team bids everyone a warm welcome. It is therefore not surprising that the Roman chapter of the Donne del Vino association, a network of women who work in the wine industry, has selected this venue as their meeting place and often hold their wine tastings here.

The dynamic design, the glass and the red colours of the restaurant's interior are reminiscent of its pre-vious life as a car showroom. The Alfa Romeo is traditionally considered to be the car of choice for Romans, and its Spider, especially in bright red, is still viewed as one of the world's great sports cars. The floor, counters and shelves in the long, gener-

Section · Floor plan
Scale 1:200

1 Entrance/shop
2 Bread bar
3 Food bar
4 Wine bar
5 Dining area
6 Tasting room
7 Kitchen

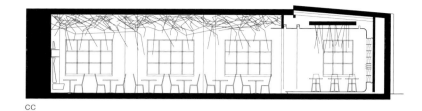

cc

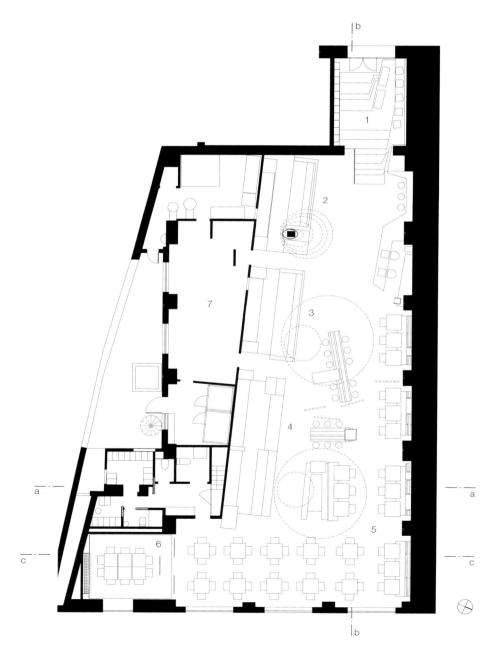

ously proportioned room are angular and oblong. The warm colour of the oak wood and the brown-washed, unplastered walls contrast with the glass of the railings and display cases as well as the polished concrete floor.

The most eye-catching feature, however, is the light fixtures. Hundreds of bent metal pipes that have been painted white and have halogen lamps fastened to their ends hang from the ceiling. Dotted in between them hang large, oval light fixtures, the wire frames of which are covered with white Lycra. The design of the two big red skylights is reminiscent of extractor hoods – a reminder of the work being performed in the kitchen. The small spotlights in the metal light fixtures twinkle like a night sky, while the cloth-covered light fixtures in between them look almost as if they are floating and cast a subdued light. The entire light installation has an organic structure. The metal rods and ovals appear to be swarming under the ceiling like microorganisms. Small organisms are an indispensable part of winemaking and also baking.

The glass reflects the light, and the entire room is bathed in light without being too bright. The dominant colours, brown and red, create an inviting atmosphere and a truly appetising ambience. There is a perfect synthesis between old and new materials, cold and warm, technical and organic. Magical, dynamic and emotional – these three aspects coalesce in this locality, the magic of which quickly enchants all who come here.

winecenter in Kaltern (Italy)

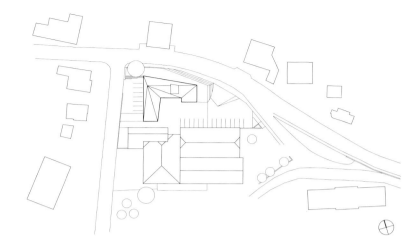

Architects: klein architekten, Römerstraße 72, 1070 Vienna,
Austria, www.feld72.at
Team: Gerhard Mair, Benoît Vandenbulcke, Henning Grahn
Site area: 4,142 m²
Completed: 2006
Wine-producing region: South Tyrol
Contact: winecenter, Bahnhofstraße 7, 39052 Kaltern, Italy,
www.winecenter.it

The Kaltern winery is one of the oldest and most traditional companies on the South Tyrolean Wine Route. Founded in 1906, it today has over 400 members who cultivate almost 300 hectares of vine-yards, making the cellars to one of the most important wine companies in Italy. Cooperatives in South Tyrol have a long history and traditionally represent a key economic sector in the region. For centuries, the Kaltern winery has focused on steadily improving the quality of its wines. Wines from 60 individual vineyards around Lake Kaltern and the plateau at the foot of the Mendel mountains (which offer ideal growing conditions due to their loose, chalky gravel soil) are produced here today.

To mark the occasion of its 100th anniversary in 2006, it was intended that the company should have a sparkling new image. It had become increasingly apparent that offering good wines

alone were no longer enough when it came to modern marketing. According to the chairman at the time, Armin Dissertori, who himself has a great interest in architecture, an invitation to bid on the construction of a new sales outlet and event venue on the premises of the winery was submitted to the South Tyrolean Architects Association in 2005. The architects practice feld72 in Vienna succeeded in winning the bid. Five architects, led by Michael Obrist, were involved in the process. The mission was to build a free-standing wine shop on the square in front of the existing building, which dates back to 1911. On the one hand, the new building was to be an attention-grabber, but on the other, it was not to obscure the existing building. Both sides exchanged ideas and thoughts during joint on-site inspections. Planning began in May 2005, and construction started in October of the same year. The celebration to mark the opening had already been planned for the spring of 2006, so time was of the essence.
In the short period and with a relatively small budget, the architects created a building of mono-lithic character. The space between the existing, more than 100-year-old building and the new sales outlet not only provides space for parking but, most importantly, also serves as a cosy inner courtyard. Visitors can linger where the two sections of the L-shaped, new building meet and enjoy a glass of wine or cup of coffee. The winecenter is not only a place where wine is sold and events are held – it is also a village café and place to meet. Located at

the entrance to the village and with an openness created by the large floor-to-ceiling glass windows, it invites not only the people of Kaltern to visit but also tourists at this popular holiday region.
The different heights of the monolithic new building provide a point of reference not only to the existing building erected in 1911 but also to the mountains beyond, which in turn are reflected in the glass elements of the building. Only when up close does one realise that the façade is not made of wood but rather of glass fibre reinforced concrete blocks that have been tinted dark brown. From all three sides, the large glass corners provide a view of the build-ing's interior.
This is where a single open space with four equally open, terraced levels can be found. The sales out-let is located on the ground floor. Rectangular blocks of solid wood – with depressions for the wine bottles carved into their surfaces – serve both to store and display the wines; detailed information about the products is provided on the blocks for all those interested. In addition, a rectangular recess, which is lit from below and covered with glass, offers information about the region and the location of the vineyards. All the elements are made from acacia wood, which is abundant in South Tyrol – not only the display blocks for the winery's wines but also the shelving used to display regional speci-alities such as delicatessen items, liqueurs and spirits. Even the large till and packaging table next to the entrance is made of solid acacia wood from the region. Customers can taste wines from the

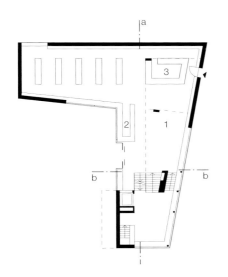
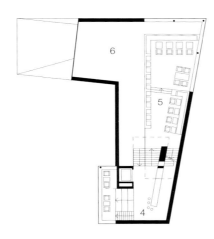
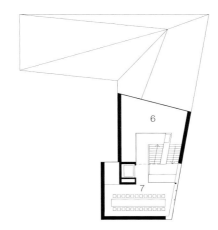

Site plan
Scale 1:2,000
Floor plan
Scale 1:500

1 Sales area
2 Tills
3 Degustation
4 Wine bar
5 Lounge
6 Air space
7 Tasting room

classic line, the wine selections, the Solos biodynamic project and the Pfarrhof and Castel Gio-
vanelli wine estates at the large tasting counter.

In contrast to the furniture, simple, polished flowing
concrete was selected for the floor. The terraced,
almost free-floating levels and the ceiling are made
of fair-faced concrete. Rare wines and more mature
wines can be found on an intermediate level above
the cellar. A concrete staircase leads from the sales
room to the mezzanine, where wines from the Baron
di Pauli wine estate are displayed. The grapes from
the Arzenhof vineyard – a centuries' old vineyard
situated high above Lake Kaltern, in the middle of
one of Europe's most beautiful wine estates – and
from the Höfl unterm Stein vineyard are vinified for
the Baron Di Pauli family at the Kaltern winery.

An open wooden staircase leads to the first floor,
where the wine bar is situated. The lounge,
designed as a gallery, floats above the sales room.
This is where a glass of wine or other beverages
can be enjoyed while taking in a view of the ground
floor or the picturesque village, which can be seen
through the floor-to-ceiling windows. The warm
colours of the wood panelling on the inside of the
balustrade and the acacia floor create a relaxing
atmosphere. This area is also rented out for parties
or corporate events; if desired, a caterer will provide
the right food to complement the wine. The decor
of the tast-ing room situated above is all white. The
bright, neutral atmosphere promotes the concen-

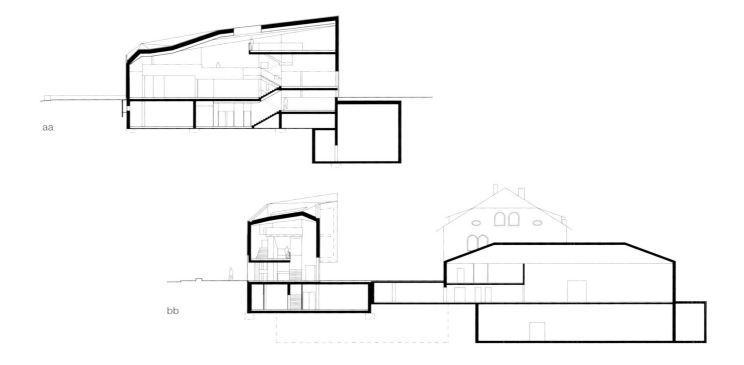

aa

bb

tration needed to evaluate wine objectively. The only element of colour is provided by the square canvases at the back of the room, which represent the different wine flavours in terms of colour.

The open, angular structure of the building is designed for exploration. The different levels project like oriel windows into the space, which seems light, airy and transparent as a result of its many glass components. Simple, top-quality wooden furniture and colourful upholstered armchairs add a nice touch, as well as the paintings and installations by the artists Andrea Varesco and Josef Rainer, whose works create a point of reference to the history of the region. Everywhere there are opportunities to look, obtain information and taste products – or simply pause to allow the space to make an impression: the seat cushions on the stairs, for example, extend an invitation to linger. The architects succeeded in conveying a sense of elegance using relatively simple yet top-quality materials. The way in which the wine is displayed is sophisticated but at the same time down-to-earth.
The winecenter is open daily, even on weekends –

something that is very rare in the region. It has an extremely competent staff, all of whom have an excellent knowledge of the wines of the region, especially as many of the wine consultants themselves grow wine and fruit as a sideline. In addition, wine-themed events are held approximately every two months: hikes through the vineyards, Night of the Open Wine Cellars or exhibitions, to name just a few. And of course regular tours of the ancient, vaulted wine cellars in the original building are conducted.

Customers include both local regular guests and tourists. But the project also met with an impressive response from experts, which means that architects frequently arrive to take a look at the building.
On 24 June 2006, the opening festivities were held as part of the centenary celebrations. Although several local residents and members of the cooperative needed a bit of time to become accustomed to the modern building, everyone was pleasantly surprised by its beauty and quality once they took a closer look and visit inside.

Appendix

The Folly Bar in London (UK)

Architects: Fusion Design & Architecture LLP,
4 Risborough Street, London SE1 0HE, UK,
www.fusiondna.co.uk
Completed: 2010
Contact: The Folly, 41 Gracechurch Street,
London EC3V 0BT, UK, www.thefollybar.co.uk

The name of the "Folly Bar" restaurant – "folly" essentially means "madness" or "silliness" – is derived from a term used in landscape gardening and refers architectural structures that turn wishful thinking into something concrete. The garden theme is echoed throughout the restaurant, which extends over two floors, in a variety of out-of-the-ordinary ways. First of all, there is the 8 m-high trunk of a Norwegian spruce "growing" through the two storeys. But there are also other objects that echo the theme, from potted plants to the small flower shop that is part of the overall concept. All the dining areas, which can accommodate 500 people, are dominated by an unconventional blend of designs created by the interiors and architecture agency Fusion Design & Architecture. The restaurateurs Drake & Morgan offer something to suit every taste and every occasion, but above all they offer a unique ambience that can best be described as a combination of lounge, wine bar, restaurant and private library. The repertoire in the dining areas is correspondingly varied, offering architecturally diverse, botanically inspired settings.

Negozio Classica in London (UK)

Architects: designLSM, The Bath House,
58 Livingstone Road, Hove BN3 3WL, UK
www.designlsm.com
Completed: 2012
Contact: Negozio Classica, 154 Regent's Park Road,
Primrose Hill, London NW1 8XN, UK,
www.negozioclassica.co.uk

The Avignonesi winery from Montepulciano has succeeded in showcasing Tuscan wine and food at authentically British venues in two different parts of London. Two localities, the interior and exterior of which could not be more authentic, were selected for this purpose: picturesque Notting Hill, where the first wine shop and wine bar was launched in 2002 and, 10 years later, fashionable Primrose Hill, where a wine shop and restaurant was opened under the same name. In both cases, the facades, which have been left untouched, signal unconventional hospitality, implemented inside by designLSM as a lively combination of wine shop and wine bar, complemented by several colourful and stylish displays.

Hedonism Wines in London (UK)

Shop design: Management team, Hedonism
Lighting designers: Speirs and Major, 8 Shepherdess Walk,
London N1 7LB, UK, www.speirsandmajor.com
Completed: 2012
Contact: Hedonism Wines, 3–7 Davies St., London W1K
3LD, UK, www.hedonism.co.uk

This wine shop is unique in every respect. From its name to its huge selection (5,500 wines and 2,000 spirits ranging in price from £15 to £120,000), the staff (a dozen salesmen and women who together speak 10 different languages) to owner Yevgeny Chichvarkin – a Russian oligarch who moved to London from Moscow. Having previously tried in vain to invest several million pounds in the traditional British wine trade, he has now created his own superlative wine shop with uniquely showcased, complete collections of the world's most famous wines, a temperature controlled-basement built especially for the wine stored there, a huge chandelier fashioned from 125 upended, handblown Riedel wine glasses and even a children's play area.

Weingut Neef-Emmich in Bermersheim (Germany)

Architects: klein architekten, Römerstraße 10,
55257 Budenheim, Germany, www.klein-architekten.com
Completed: 2011
Wine-producing region: Rheinhessen
Contact: Weingut Neef-Emmich, Alzeyer Straße 15,
67593 Bermersheim, Germany, www.neef-emmich.de

It is rare to see a redesigned "Kuhkapelle" (cow chapel) – another name for the traditional vaulted barns which are now a characteristic feature of building and wine culture in Rheinhessen – that is so flawless, unostentatious and beautiful. During the course of remodelling, which was performed in two stages, a tasting room measuring 45 m^2 was created in a former barn in Bermersheim, Rhineland-Palatinate, the minimalistic fixtures and fittings of which impressively make reference to the historic fabric of the building. Use was made not only of colours related to winegrowing but also of building materials and other elements such as oak wood, mineral-rich earth and limestone. In striking contrast to the bright ambience, which emphasizes the materials, and the sleek, dark furniture, the space and the presentation of the wine estate's products captivate visitors with a straightforward and uncontrived style.

WeinKulturgut Longen-Schlöder in Longuich (Germany)

Architects: Matteo Thun & Partners, Via Appiani 9,
I–20121 Milan
Completed: 2013
Wine-producing region: Mosel
Contact: WeinKulturgut Longen-Schlöder, Kirchenweg 9,
54340 Longuich, Germany, www.longen-schloeder.de

When it came time to expand their wine estate, Sabine and Markus Longen not only wanted to create a new conference building but also overnight accommodation for their guests, who frequently came from far away. They were able to persuade the South Tyrolian architect Matteo Thun to create an overall concept. Inspired by the size and design of the small wooden huts typically found in the vineyards of the Mosel region, which offer refuge from bad weather and space to store tools, 20 small guest cottages – rather than one single building – were created in cooperation with the firm of architects Stein, Hemmes, Wirtz. The use of local slate is characteristic of the exterior of the cottages – a reminder of the vineyard walls typical for the Mosel region. Each building has its own individually designed small garden with table and chairs. "We want to show what living in harmony with nature should look like," say Sabine and Markus Longen.

Each of the cottages – created, as the website states, "for the fine art of doing nothing" – offers space for a generously proportioned room and modern bathroom. Warm colours were used for the deliberately simplistic fixtures and fittings. Like the vineyard huts on the Mosel, the dominant material is wood from local oak trees, complemented by country-style textiles and beautifully handcrafted decorative details.

Weingut Franz Keller in Oberbergen (Germany)

Architects: Geis & Brantner, Gartenstraße 23,
79098 Freiburg, Germany,
www.geis-brantner.de
Completed: 2013
Wine-producing region: Baden
Contact: Weingut Franz Keller, Badbergstraße 23
79235 Vogtsburg im Kaiserstuhl, Germany,
www.franz-keller.de

As a pioneer of fully fermented German wine, Franz Keller ranks among Baden's iconic winemakers. He became popular with the dry wines he produces and the famous French wines imports and stores not far from his award-winning "Schwarzer Adler" restaurant. His son Fritz expanded these mainstays of the Keller empire by adding a modern architectural component: a terraced new building was created in Riedental in Oberbergen and nestles harmoniously in the cultivated landscape of the Kaiserstuhl. The 4,000-m² "green building", equipped with state-of-the-art technology, was built according to plans drawn up by the architects Michael Geis and Ulrich Brantner. A restaurant and equally light-filled, sleekly designed tasting room and sales space situated next to the large production facilities, which extend over three levels, offer an impressive view of the Kaiserstuhl's terraced vineyards.

neues-weinkaufen.de in Ratingen (Germany)

Designer: Guido Hellmann, Oberstrasse 27, 40878 Ratingen, Germany
Carpenter: Waldemar Morlang, Am Gratenpoet 3b, 40878 Ratingen, Germany
Completed: 2010
Contact: Guido Hellmann, Oberstrasse 27, 40878 Ratingen, Germany
www.neues-weinkaufen.de

Nomen est omen: "Grandpa's wine shop is out". It is not only winemakers who have discovered the opportunities for raising one's profile that high-quality contemporary architecture and individualised design offer. Wine merchants are also setting new standards with the way their outlets are designed, thus ensuring that they stand out from the often monotonous, run-of-the-mill displays at large companies. A perfect example is this new wine shop, founded in 2009, with its light-filled ambience. Purple boards with handwritten information about the wines, which hang above the displays, are the only splash of colour among the light-coloured fixtures and fittings. The shop's design is pleasantly streamlined, with the wines displayed in tubes, thus ensuring that customers are not overwhelmed by a confusing range of products but instead can easily navigate the selection with the help of good advice.

Weinsinn in Frankfurt (Germany)

Restaurant designer: Milica Trajkovska Scheiber, Fürstenbergerstraße 179, 60322 Frankfurt am Main, Germany
Completed: 2009
Contact: Weinsinn Restaurant & Catering, Fürstenbergerstraße 179, 60322 Frankfurt am Main, Germany,
www.weinsinn-frankfurt.de

As is often the case with this metropolis on the Main river, a corner building in the northern Westend district, built in a style typical for the late 19th century, serves up a surprise – both visually and from a food perspective. An outside staircase leads first to a small covered terrace, then to the bistro and the wine bar, which with a retro 1950s-inspired design constitute a happy blend of unpretentious restaurant and strikingly colourful gallery ambience. Thanks in part to its interior, which is typical of the period and boasts authentic furniture, Weinsinn has become a popular place to eat, where the owner has skilfully implemented a "bistronomics" concept.

Glas.Cabinet, Weingut Robert Weil in Kiedrich (Germany)

Architects: Planungsbüro Heiko Preusser, 65399 Kiedrich, Germany
Tasting area: eins:33 GmbH, Dreimühlenstraße 19, 80469 Munich, Germany, www.einszu33.com
Completed: 2013
Wine-producing region: Rheingau
Contact: Weingut Robert Weil, Mühlberg 5, 65399 Kiedrich/ Rheingau, Germany www.weingut-robert-weil.com

It is extremely rare for a wine estate to afford itself the luxury of maintaining not just one but two wine shops. This unusual constellation can be found at one of the world's most renowned Riesling wine estates. Fifteen years ago, Wilhelm Weil opened his first, postmodern wine shop, which complements the architecturally interesting Tudor-style villa dating back to the 19th century, and its outbuildings. With the completion in 2013 of the winery's new building, designed to ensure optimum production processes, the Glas.Cabinet, an additional visitor facility is, in a manner of speaking, its crowning glory. Complete with a terrace, this is where large groups of guests can also be accommodated comfortably. The sleek, elegant pavilion, characterised by blue-black natural stone and pale oak wood, not only boasts state-of-the-art gastronomic technology but also a large expanse of glass that provides panoramic views of the surrounding vineyards.

Rotisserie Weingrün in Berlin (Germany)

Restaurant designer: Herbert Beltle, Heide Hagen
Completed: 2009
Contact: rotisserie WEINGRÜN, Gertraudenstraße 10–12, 10178 Berlin, Germany, www.rotisserie-weingruen.de

The listed neogothic "Juwel-Palais" – with its richly ornamented sandstone facade, the only existing three-gabled building in Berlin – is situated on a side arm of the Spree in central Berlin. It underwent extensive renovation in 2002. The restaurateur Herbert Beltle – also owner of the Horcher wine estate in Rheinland-Palatinate (which includes an exquisite showroom) – has created a combination grill/wine restaurant which boasts a wall-mounted rotisserie grill and a remarkable selection of wine and food.

Original features, such as ceilings, tiled floors and large windows, have been retained and provide a framework for the bistro-style design. A striking feature is the large, indirectly lit wine and display rack and the dark-coloured walls on which slates featuring the dishes of the day hang.

Weinmanufaktur Untertürkheim in Stuttgart (Germany)

Architects: Wolfgang Münzing Innenarchitekt, Neubrunnenstraße 23, 74223 Flein, Germany, www.wolfgang-muenzing.de
Completed: 2011
Contact: Weinmanufaktur Untertürkheim, Strümpfelbacher Straße 47, 70327 Stuttgart, Germany, www.weinmanufaktur.de

Treading new paths – that is and was the motto when it came time for these winegrowers, whose ancestors joined forces to create a cooperative in 1887, to choose a new name. In 2001, the cooperative changed its name to "Weinmanufaktur". The company's more than 100-year-old building was also imbued with new architectural lustre, with spacious tasting and sales rooms spanned by three flat arches and dotted with "tasting islands" as well as stylish room dividers and display elements. In place of trendy gimmicks, bright gold-varnished surfaces and elegantly curved counters made of ash prevail, giving the large wine shop a discreetly elegant ambience and focusing attention on the sensual experience that wine offers.

BECKER'S XO in Trier (Germany)

Architects: Atelier d'Architecture et de Design Jim Clemes,
120, rue de Luxembourg, 4221 Esch/Alzette, Luxembourg
www.clemes.lu
Completed: 2013
Contact: BECKER'S XO, Fleischstraße 59,
Posthof am Kornmarkt, 54290 Trier, Germany,
www.xo-trier.de

BECKER'S XO, which opened in 2013 in a building complex located directly at the Kornmarkt in Trier that previously served as a post office, is a perfect blend of restaurant, bar and deli. The post and telegraph building, the construction of which commenced in 1879, was remodelled after the postal distribution centre was closed and is gradually being populated with shops, restaurants, bars and flats. In collaboration with the firm of architects Jim Clemes, the client and Trier gourmet chef Wolfgang Becker has, in XO, achieved a cross-over concept on 700 m² of space. The individual areas have different characters, depending on the purpose for which they are being used, but together they create a unit.

The remodelling left the neo-baroque facade of the listed building complex untouched; only the windows facing the inner courtyard were extended down to the ground to create a more immediate connection to the newly created courtyard, which also serves as a terrace for XO.

Inside, the existing, in parts rugged, structure and particular charm of the rooms were retained and complemented by new, clear lines and exclusive materials. There are almost no full-length walls dividing up the overall space. Instead, free-standing metal walls with surfaces made of treated black sheet metal are used to delineate the different areas. They also constitute an element that is repeated in the individual food-related spaces and acts as a link between the areas, which have otherwise been designed differently in line with the function they serve.

Wein und Wahrheit in Sulzbach (Germany)

Architects: Ippolito Fleitz Group GmbH, identity architects
Augustenstraße 87, 70197 Stuttgart, Germany,
www. ifgroup.org
Completed: 2011
Contact: Wein und Wahrheit, Weinkellerei Höchst GmbH,
Main-Taunus-Zentrum, 65843 Sulzbach/Taunus, Germany,
www.weinkellerei-hoechst.de

Like a library filled with books, wine bottles fill the store from floor to ceiling along all three interior walls. The light breaks through a canopy of glass orbs suspended from the ceiling like candlelight reflected through a glass. A mirrored ceiling band running around the edges of the space makes the room appear higher than it actually is. A mere 85 m² of space was available in the new extension of the Main-Taunus Centre for the well-known Weinkellerei Höchst's second wine shop. The mission was to present its range of over 600 different wines and spirits, delicatessen items and gifts within this compact space. The facade was pulled slightly inward to optimise the space; at the same time, the concave entrance area attracts attention and invites passers-by to enter the store. Glass and oak are the dominant materials in the space, both chosen as a reference to the world of wine. They create a sensual ambience, which appeals to bon vivants who attach great importance to quality when making a decision to buy.

Georg Hack – Haus der Guten Weine in Meersburg (Germany)

Architects: Bühler und Bühler, Lindwurmstraße 88, 80337 München, Germany, www.buehler-buehler.de
Completed: 2007
Contact: Georg Hack – Haus der Guten Weine GmbH & Co. KG, Schützenstraße 1, 88709 Meersburg, Germany, www.georg-hack.com

When Georg Hack opened his shop in 1951 in Meersburg's old town, his portfolio comprised only a couple hundred different wines. During the course of the intervening decades, this portfolio has been continually expanded to include new wines. Ultimately, customer traffic, which had steadily increased since the 1980s, also created an urgent need for new premises. A generously proportioned new building was created on top of a vaulted cellar in 2007. Ever since then, the exquisite selection of wines has been presented in an all-white, modern wine gallery which extends over two floors connected by a striking staircase. The wines – approximately 1,000 in number – are displayed in 400 niches and flank the large, minimalistically designed interior, which is used for a wide variety of different events, in a neat and inviting manner.

Bella Italia Weine in Stuttgart (Germany)

Architects: Ippolito Fleitz Group GmbH, identity architects, Augustenstraße 87, 70197 Stuttgart, Germany, www.ifgroup.org
Completed: 2007
Contact: Bella Italia Weine, Vogelsangstraße 18, 70176 Stuttgart, Germany, www.bella-italia-weine.de

Although the name might suggest otherwise, "Bella Italia" is the opposite of the romantic kitsch restaurant cliché. The restaurant, housed in a building dating back to the late 19th century, differs from standard restaurant design solutions as a result of its creative fixtures and fittings and tasteful colour palette. The aim was to create a place with different sections reflecting the character of the owner Maria Patané – a collector and storyteller.
The ceilings and walls have all been painted the same dark olive green, and off-white wainscoting encompasses the entire room. On the left, next to the entrance, attention is focused on the ceiling with its more than 90 different mirrors that continually open up new perspectives and reflect the light from the ceiling lights. Mauve chairs and tables laid with white tablecloths provide a striking contrast to the light-coloured parquet flooring. The same chairs can also be found in the right-hand section of the restaurant. Here, however, it is a long, oval table – reminiscent of the table in a parlour – that is, together with the wide variety of different old and new pendant lamps, the dominant feature.

Weingut F. J. Regnery in Klüsserath (Germany)

Architects: marcohoffmann.architektur, Mozartstraße 34, 54516 Wittlich, Germany, www.mhar.de
Completed: 2013
Wine-producing region: Mosel
Contact: Weingut F. J. Regnery, Mittelstraße 39, 54340 Klüsserath, Germany, www.regnery.kreakom.de

The new Regnery wine shop in the seemingly placid village of Klüsserath is a real eye-catcher, evoking many different connotations or even feelings of bemusement. It is quite unique and, at first glance, appears to have nothing in common with the neighbouring, 19th-century buildings commonly found in the Mosel region. The vertical, red-brown oak cladding of the new oval structure, situated in a courtyard paved with grey cobblestones, underscores the contrast. The new building offers spectacular views of the renowned Klüsserather Bruderschaft vineyards, the wines of which can be tasted in this architecturally noteworthy and visually striking environment.

Vineyard in Eimsbüttel/Hamburg (Germany)

Furnishers / lighting designer: PLY unestablished furniture, Hohenesch 68, 22765 Hamburg, Germany, www.ply.com
Completed: 2012
Contact: Vineyard Hamburg GmbH, Osterstraße 92, 20259 Hamburg, Germany, www.vineyard-weinhandel.de

In 2012, Elke Berner and Alexander Bolognino de Orth launched their business model involving complementary lines of business on 700 m² of space in a former car repair shop situated in a rear courtyard. The business model comprises a wine bar, which offers pleasure and enjoyment in this wonderful location, and a wine shop, where wines, spirits and delicatessen items can purchased until 11 pm. The modern bar is not the only place where the 400 wines, 60 of which are available by the glass, can be enjoyed. Black armchairs and furniture made from untreated, rough-hewn wood can be found in front of the open, rust-red fireplace, which is flanked on both sides by large stacks of wood. Barrique barrels with glass tops act as tables. A long wine rack made of dark wood runs along the wall opposite the bar. The black industrial light fixtures incorporated in the overall lighting concept serve as a reminder of the building's former use.

Weingut Poss in Windesheim (Germany)

Architects: Oliver Schrögel Architekturbüro, Schwabenheimer Weg 62a, 55543 Bad Kreuznach, Germany, www.schroegel-schroegel.de
Interior designers: Planungsbüro i21, Nahestraße 16, D–55593 Rüdesheim/Nahe, www.innenarchitektur21.de
Completed: 2011
Wine-producing region: Nahe
Contact: Weingut Poss, Goldgrube 20–22, 55452 Windesheim, Germany, www.weingut-poss.de

Seldom can such an immediate link be established between traces of ancient construction and today's architecture than on the premises of the Poss brothers' wine estate, which includes sections of a Roman wine cellar. The surviving brickwork, together with wine and oil amphorae, are an historic attraction that can be found beneath a wine shop created in 2011 by Oliver Schrögel and Heiko Gruber. The name of the shop, Pinoteca, is derived from the Pinot grapes associated with the Burgundy region of France.

A burgundy-coloured and a slate wall with display niches provide colourfully appealing counterpoints within the context of the interior design, which has a light and airy feeling thanks to the tall windows and light-coloured floors and ceiling. With a bit of luck, guests will find themselves being given advice at the wine counter made from local wood by the 2013/2014 German Wine Queen, Nadine Poss, to whom the wine estate is home.

360° Café Weinbar Lounge in Innsbruck (Austria)

Architects: dominique perrault architecture, 6, rue Bouvier, 75011 Paris, France, www.perraultarchitecte.com
Completed: 2005
Contact: 360° Cafe Weinbar Lounge, Maria-Theresien-Straße 18, 6020 Innsbruck, Austria, www.360-grad.at

The Rathausgalerien shopping centre, built according to plans by Dominique Perrault, offers an impressive panoramic view over the city to the tops of the nearby mountains from its roof on the seventh floor. With the space's fully-glazed 360-degree front, which opens up to a viewing platform that spans the entire circumference, and an open design which owes a debt to the spectacular view, the interior design is the perfect complement to the visual experience – and no more so than when the sun goes down. The subdued colours and restrained design recede into the background during the day when the cityscape surrounding the building comes into its own. The rest of the time, the harmonious lighting and the warm beiges and bright yellows contribute to the aura of this locality, which is particularly popular thanks to its atmosphere and prime location.

Weinmanufaktur Strobl in Feuersbrunn (Austria)

Architect: architypen, Wolfgang Wimmer, Lessingstraße 6, 4020 Linz, Austria, www.architypen.at
Designer: MARCH GUT, Tummelplatz 1, 4020 Linz, Austria, www.marchgut.com
Completed: 2013
Contact: Weinmanufaktur Clemens Strobl, Hauptkellergasse, 3483 Feuersbrunn, Austria, www.clemens-strobl.com

The Boutique Winery Clemens Strobl in the Lower Austrian town Feuersbrunn produces premium wines from Riesling and Grüner Veltliner grapes – Austria's indigenous white grape varieties – as well as Pinot Noir. The vintner focuses on a quality that distances itself from mass production; his rich wines are intended to reflect their terroir. The new display and sales spaces were developed in a former wine cellar as an architectural flagship of the wine estate. During the one-year-long rebuilding and renovation, old parts of the building were laid bare and returned to their original state. A modern extension was also built on the upper level.

The building extends across three levels. Several steps lead from the ground floor down to the tasting area, which is fitted out in white maple wood. Adjacent to this is the 50 m-long vaulted cellar, in which the wines are stored and presented in stacks of crates in an atmospheric space. Culinary events take place on the open, light upper level. A sweeping window and the terrace afford a panoramic view of the surrounding vineyards.

Meraner Weinhaus in Meran (Italy)

Architect: Harry Thaler, 51 Tudor Road, Unit 4, London
E97SN, UK, www.harrythaler.it
Completed: 2011
Contact: Meraner Weinhaus GmbH, Romstraße 76,
39012 Meran, Italy, www.meranerweinhaus.com

Named Italy's best in *enoteca* in 2004, this wine
shop is managed by two professional sommeliers
and has, for a number of decades, excelled not
only because of its huge range of more than 2,500
wines (not to mention 500 spirits and carefully
selected delicatessen items) but also because of its
interactive wine-tasting station, where 40 different
wines from a wide variety of regions can be tasted
anytime. The "tasting zone", with its wine dispen-
sers, is therefore a special attraction and is surrounded on three sides by shelving units and wine
displays made from light and dark wood. These
harmonise pleasantly with the light-coloured floors
and ceilings and enable the bottles to be presented
in a way that best suits the product, either standing
up or lying down.

Monvínic in Barcelona (Spain)

Interior designer: Alfons Tost, Passatge Marimón, 7,
08021 Barcelona, Spain, www.alfonstost.com
Completed: 2008
Contact: Monvínic, Carrer de la Diputació, 249,
08007 Barcelona, Spain,
www.monvinic.com

Monvínic is one of the most famous addresses
for fine wine and food – not only in Barcelona but
also far beyond. It could well be referred to as an
oenological-culinary institution. The portfolio of
international wines comprises approximately
3,000 labels, 60 of which are available by the glass.
Instead of selecting wines from printed wine lists,
customers make their selection digitally using a
"WinePad" or after receiving expert advice from
one of the six sommeliers. Interior decorator Alfons
Tost designed the restaurant and wine bar as individually and impressively as he did the tasting and
conference room and the document centre. He
made use of a variety of materials – primarily wood
and various metals – and implemented an ingenious lighting concept. Gold-coloured ceilings and
light yellow wall coverings complement the elegantly contemporary sofas and chairs, upholstered
in vibrant yellows and dark browns, as well as the
beige-coloured floors – creating a kind of comprehensive work of art that speaks to all five senses.

OHLA in Barcelona (Spain)

Architects: Alonso Balaguer y Arquitectos Asociados,
Carrer de la Riba, 36, 08950 Esplugues de Llobregat, Spain
Completed: 2011
Contact: Ohla Hotel, Via Laietana, 49, 08003 Barcelona,
Spain, www.ohlahotel.com

The ceramic eye sculptures created by the artist
Frederic Amat, which gaze down from the neo-
classical facade of what was once the city's first
department store, are the first indication of the not
quite everyday style of this luxury boutique hotel,
which was opened in 2011. The design choices of
the two men responsible for the lavish and fanciful
design, Alonso Balaguer and Daniel Isern, include
exquisite furniture from the Cappellini collection
and an exceptional lighting installation by artec3, a
design studio specializing in architectural lighting
design. There is no shortage of all kinds of eye-
catching elements, as demonstrated by the fixtures
and fittings for the Boutique Bar and the Gastrobar,
with their spectacular installations and bold con-
trasts in terms of light, materials and colours.

Bodega 14 Viñas in Picón (Spain)

Architects: S-M.A.O. Sancho-Madridejos Architecture Office, Calle Santa Leonor, 61 Bajo 2A, 28037 Madrid, Spain, www.sancho-madridejos.com
Completed: 2008
Wine-producing region: La Mancha
Contact: 14 Viñas, S.L. – Viñedos y bodega en Finca Casalobos, Carretera autonómica CM 412, km 6.5, 13196 Picón, Spain

Modern wine architecture is well represented in Spain with a conspicuously large number of out-of-the-ordinary projects. This includes a wine cellar created in 2008 in the Castile-La Mancha region. Near Picón (in the province of Ciudad Real), a cube with a pleated metallic skin made of aluminium stretches across the slope of the hill – more reminiscent of an industrial building than a wine estate. The architects Juan Carlos Sancho Osinaga and Sol Madridejos, who in 2009 were nominated for the Mies van der Rohe Award on the basis of this project, housed the production facilities and wine cellar on the lower level, behind the 80 m-long facade. The upper level provides spacious, elegantly proportioned rooms of fair-faced concrete that accommodate a lounge and tasting areas, which offer spectacular views of the vineyards.

PaCatar in Seville (Spain)

Architects: Donaire Arquitectos, Calle Velarde, 10A, 41001 Seville, Spain, www.donairearquitectos.com
Completed: 2011
Contact: PaCatar, Calle Javier Lasso de la Vega, 1, 41002 Seville, Spain

At first glance, the almost spartan design of this wine restaurant, which opened in the centre of Seville in 2011, gives it the appearance of a country restaurant. Concrete floors, wood panelled and whitewashed brick walls, rustic wooden stools and simply designed chairs – the firm of architects Juan Pedro Donaire Arquitectos relied on simplicity, avoiding excess of any kind and superfluous decorative elements. The fixtures and fittings are intended to symbolise wine's connection with the earth; this concept was implemented by giving preference to natural materials. Shelves resembling wine crates mounted below the ceiling, pale green glass light fixtures with a shape reminiscent of wine glasses and slim, white, cast iron pillars add discreet design touches to the simple interior.

Finca de los Arandinos in Entrena (Spain)

Architect: Javier Arizcuren, Calle San Anton, 1–5G, 26002 Logroño, Spain
Interior designers: David Delfín, Calle Augusto Figueroa, 16 1A planta, 28004 Madrid, Spain, www.davidelfin.com; AKA ESTUDIO, Calle Duque de Osuna, 4, 28015 Madrid, Spain, www.akaestudio.com
Completed: 2011
Wine-producing region: Rioja
Contact: Finca de los Arandinos, Carretera LR-137, km 4,6, 26375 Entrena, Spain, www.fincadelosarandinos.com

This hotel, with its highly-praised restaurant, is a triumph of modern architecture. Situated in the heart of the Rioja region, the hotel was the 2013 winner of the Best of Wine Tourism award presented by the Great Wine Capitals. Together with AKA ESTUDIO, architect Javier Arizcuren and interior designer David Delfín have created a rich variety of coloured elements from materials such as concrete, glass and wood which add a fresh, cheerful note to the premises. The design not only successfully connects the hotel to the adjacent wine estate, with its barrique cellar, wine-tasting counter and wine bar, but also succeeds in showcasing the spectacular surroundings with the adjacent vineyards and orchards of the Rioja region and the mountains of the Sierra de Moncalvillo.

La Vinoteca Torres in Barcelona (Spain)

Architects: Estudi Arola, Lope de Vega 106 3er, 08005 Barcelona, Spain, www.estudiarola.com
Completed: 2008
Contact: Vinoteca Torres – Restaurant de Vins, Passeig de Gràcia, 78, 08008 Barcelona, Spain, www.lavinotecatorres.com

Having opened a modern wine shop in 2005 in the La Roca Village shopping outlet, not far from Barcelona, as the first culinary ambassador for his renowned wine empire, Miguel Torres established another venue three years later at the heart of the Catalonian metropolis that embodies an upscale culinary concept in which wine takes pride of place. Several dozen Torres wines are served – also by the glass – in the wine bar and in the restaurant, with its sophisticated cuisine. The striking contrast between the light wood furniture and the surrounding dark-coloured walls and subdued lighting creates a dramatic effect, which – like the first Torres wine shop – is an integral aspect of the design concept created by the design studio Estudi Arola.

Weingut Schmid Wetli in Berneck (Switzerland)

Architects: Bänzigers Architektur AG, Kirchgasse 1,
9442 Berneck, Switzerland, www.baenzigersarchitektur.ch
Completed: 2010
Wine-producing region: St. Gallen
Contact: Schmid Wetli AG, Tramstraße 23, 9442 Berneck,
Switzerland, www.schmidwetli.ch

Examples of contemporary wine architecture remain rare in Switzerland. The wine estate belonging to the Schmid and Wetli winemaking families is one of the few estates in the Rhine Valley in the past few years to decide in favour of a modern design when it became time to erect new buildings. A wine-pressing room, barrel cellar and tasting room were created in several stage of construction, all supervised by Bänzigers Architektur AG. The cantilevered tasting room is just one of the interesting architectural features that the 300-m² hall, clad with untreated Douglas fir slats and oxidised steel bands, has to offer. Furnished with dark-coloured furniture, the wood-panelled wine tasting room provides insights into the winemaking process and views of the adjacent vineyards of the canton of St. Gallen.

Sushibar+Wine in Helsinki (Finland)

Interior designers: Eliisa Korpijarvi, Pursimiehenkatu 2 LH 3,
00150 Helsinki, Finland, www.eliisakorpijarvi.com
Completed: 2010
Contact: Sushibar+Wine FREDA, Fredrikinkatu 42,
00100 Helsinki, Finland, www.sushibar.fi

Wine, sushi and distinctive Scandinavian design characterise the success of several new speciality restaurants in the Finnish capital. The Sushibar + Wine restaurants opened in the centre of Helsinki by the two wine merchants Anders Westerholm und Matti Sarkkinen – "The We Are Group" – are impressive not only because of their remarkable and extensive portfolio of wines (50 types) but also their sharp, clean design. The person behind it is Eliisa Korpijarvi, who selected furniture designed by Alvar Aalto, considered one of the pioneers of modern interior design. The emphasis placed on the contrast between light and dark when it came to the shelves, benches and tables made from pine and birch creates a quietly rustic, subtle interior that harmonises visually with the Japanese cuisine and the wines that accompany it.

Drop Shop wine bar in Budapest (Hungary)

Interior designers: suto interior architects, Ötvös János utcában 1b, 1021 Budapest, Hungary, www.suto.hu
Completed: 2010
Contact: Drop Shop, Balassi Bálint utca 27, 1055 Budapest,
Hungary, www.dropshop.hu

Light green and black are the predominant colours of the wine bar. The walls were left unplastered, the ceiling was painted black, and steel plates were selected as flooring, giving the entire space an industrial character. The lighting accentuates the bar counter and the shelves that display the wines for sale. The fixtures and fittings are mostly minimalist: all the chairs and stools are also light green or black, and wine crates have been converted into tables. The available wines and daily specials, which change regularly, are written on small boards.

The brief for architects Kata and Laszlo Suto was clear: the focus was on enjoying wine. Moreover, the project had to be implemented on a very small budget. Otherwise the two architects were not subject to any design constraints. The words "tasting zone" on the large front window say it all: more than 400 wines, including more than 60 Hungarian wines, can be tasted and purchased here.

Additional projects

Germany
- Weinkellerei Julius Kimmle, Agnes-Kimmle-Str 1, 76889 Kapellen-Drusweiler, www.kimmle-wein.de
- Winzergenossenschaft Vier Jahreszeiten Winzer eG, Limburgstr. 8, 67098 Bad Dürkheim, www.vj-wein.de
- Weingut Matthias Müller, Mainzer Str. 45, 56322 Spay, www.weingut-matthiasmueller.de
- Weingut Karl May, Ludwig-Schwamb-Straße 22, 67574 Osthofen, www.weingut-karl-may.de
- Par Terre, Georg-Friedrich-Dentzel-Straße 11, 76829 Landau, www.par-terre.de
- Barolo & Friends, Stolzestr. 40, 30171 Hanover, www.baroloandfriends.com
- Vintage-Selection, Westermühlstr. 39, 80469 Munich, www.vintage-selection.de
- Weinmuseum Köln, Amsterdamer Str. 1, 50668 Cologne, www.weinmuseum.org

Great Britain
- New Street Wine Shop, 16 New Street, London EC2M 4TR, www.newstreetwineshop.co.uk
- Vinopolis, 1 Bank End, London SE1 9BU, www. vinopolis.co.uk

Italy
- Kellerei St. Pauls, Schloss-Warth-Weg 21, 39050 San Paolo/Eppan, www.kellereistpauls.com
- Feinkost Lanz, Pustertalerstraße 7/A, 39040 Sciaves/Bressanone, www.lanz-suedtirol.it
- vinzenz – zum feinen wein, Via Città Nuova 4, 39049 Vipiteno, www.vinzenz.it
- Vinus, Altenmarktgasse 6, 39042 Bressanone, www.vinothekvinus.it

Austria
- Heurigenweingut Frühwirth, Wiener Neustädter Straße 75, 2524 Teesdorf, www.heurigenweingut.at
- Weingut Kolkmann, Flugplatzstraße 11–12, 3481 Fels am Wagram, www.kolkmann.at

- Weingut Herbert Schabl, Kremser Str. 13, 3465 Königsbrunn am Wagram, www.weingut-schabl.at
- Vinothek im Bergresort Werfenweng, Weng 195, 5453 Werfenweng, www.travelcharme.com
- Loisium Wine & Spa Resort Südsteiermark, Am Schlossberg 1a, 8461 Ehrenhausen, www.loisium.com/suedsteiermark

Spain
- Vegamar Selección, Carrer de Colón, 37, 46004 València, www.vegamarseleccion.es
- Jaleo Vinoteca, Rúa Galera, 43–45, 15003 A Coruña
- Vinoteca Blas, Calle de San José de Mayo, 5, 24700 Astorga, www.restauranteblas.es
- Restaurante Jaleo, Calle Narváez 26, 28009 Madrid und Calle Mayor 4, 28013 Madrid, www.restaurantejaleo.com
- Tanins Vinoteca, Carrer d'Arnes, 11, 43500 Tortosa, www.taninsvinoteca.com
- La Enoteca, Hotel Pesquera, Calle de la Estación, 1, 47300 Peñafiel, www.hotelpesquera.com
- Museo Provincial del Vino, Castillo de Peñafiel, 47300 Peñafiel, www.museodelvinodevalladolid.es

France
- La Bordeauxthèque, Galeries Lafayette, 35 Boulevard Haussmann, 75009 Paris, www.bordeauxtheque.com
- Cité des civilisations du vin, 7 Rue Duffour Dubergier, 33000 Bordeaux (opening 2016)

Greece
- Scala Vinoteca, Sina 50, Athens 10672, www.scalavinoteca.com
- Pantheon 1900, Kriezotou & Boudouri 22, 34100 Chalkida, www.pantheon-1900.gr

Hungary
- Somló Wine Cellars, main road No 8, 47°7'14.94" N/17°22'34.997" O, 8481 Somlóvásárhely, www.somloi.hu

Slovenia
- Rožmarin, Gosposka ulica 8, 2000 Maribor, www.rozmarin.si

- Restaurant/hotel
- Wine merchants
- Wine shop/merchants at source
- Exhibitions

Index of names

Picture credits

The authors and publishers would like to express their sincere gratitude to all those who have assisted in the production of this book, be it through providing photos or artwork or granting permission to reproduce their documents or providing other information. Photographs not specifically credited are taken from the archives of architects or of the magazine *DETAIL Review of Architecture*. Despite intensive endeavours, we were unable to establish copyright ownership in just a few cases; however, copyright is assured. Please notify us accordingly in such instances.

Cover
Andreas Lerchl, D–Stuttgart

Foreword/Indroduction
p. 6	Eugeni Pons, E–Lloret
p. 10 (left)	Marie-Lan Nguyen / Wikimedia Commons
p. 10 (right)	Heiko Gruber, D–Rüdesheim an der Nahe
p. 11	Wikimedia Commons
p. 12 (left)	Auerbachs Keller, D–Leipzig
p. 12 (centre)	Weingut Robert Weil, D–Kiedrich
p. 12 (right)	I.W. Wolff GmbH & Co. KG, D–Leer
p. 13 (top)	ullstein bild, D–Berlin
pp. 13 (bottom), 14, 15, 17	Heinz-Gert Woschek, D–Mainz
p. 16	Adnan Pjanic / www.adamantonadrian.wordpress.com
p. 18 (top)	Pepe Franco, E–Madrid
p. 18 (bottom)	GAP Interiors / Julien Fernandez
p. 19	Enoteca Italiana, I–Siena
p. 21	Fernando Guerra, P–Lisbon
p. 22	Zooey Braun, D–Stuttgart
p. 23 (left)	Weinkeller-Profi, D–Wiesbaden
p. 23 (right)	Marcus Zumbansen, D–Berlin

Projects
pp. 26, 27	Zsolt Batár, H–Budapest
pp. 28, 29	DiVino, H–Budapest
pp. 30–33	Arne Jennard, B–Antwerp
pp. 34, 35	AI photography, CZ–Prague
pp. 36–38	Christian Schittich, D–Munich
pp. 39, 40, 41 (bottom)	Lia Vittone Photography, GB–Lymington
p. 41 (top)	28°–50° Wine Workshop and Kitchen, GB–London
pp. 42, 43	René Rötheli, CH–Baden
pp. 44, 45	Christine Müller, CH–La Chaux-de-Fonds
pp. 46–49	Susanne Sommerfeld, D–Constance
pp. 50, 51	Jens Pfisterer, D–Leinfelden-Echterdingen
pp. 52, 53, 54 (bottom), 55	Rainer Diehl/h7photo.com, D–Mannheim
p. 54 (top)	Eva Feldmann, D–Mannheim
pp. 56–59	Dietmar Strauß, D–Besigheim
pp. 60–63	Zooey Braun, D–Stuttgart
pp. 64, 65	Rüdiger Mosler, D–Nochem
pp. 66–69	Andreas Lerchl, D–Stuttgart
pp. 70–73	Balthasar Ress wineBANK, D–Hattenheim
pp. 74, 75	Erich Francois, D–Cologne
pp. 76–79	José Campos, P–Porto

p. 80	Meritxell Arjalaguer, E–Barcelona
p. 81	Sascha Odermann, D–Munich
pp. 82, 83	Mikel Uribetxeberria, E–Azkoitia
pp. 84, 85	Marcin Ratajczak, PL–Poznań
pp. 86–89	Daniele Ansidei, D–Berlin
p. 90	Ingo Pertramer, A–Vienna
p. 91	Philipp Kreidel, A–Vienna
pp. 92–94	Andreas Burghardt, A–Vienna
pp. 96, 97	Dim Balsem, NL–Amsterdam
pp. 98–101	Cosmin Dragomir, RO–Bucharest
pp. 102, 103, 110, 111, 113 (bottom), 114	Günter Richard Wett, A–Innsbruck
pp. 104, 106 (top), 108 (right)	Pietro Savorelli, I–Florence
pp. 105, 106 (centre)	Leonardo Finotti, BR–São Paulo
pp. 106 (bottom), 107, 108 (left), 109	Marchesi Antinori Archive, I–Florence
pp. 112, 113 (top)	Renè Riller, I–Laudes
p. 115	Alois Lageder, I–Magé
pp. 116–119	Francesco Galli, I–Viterbo
pp. 120–123	Hertha Hurnaus, A–Vienna

Thumbnail portraits
p. 126	Media Wisdom Photography Ltd, GB–Shepperton
p. 127 (left)	Negozio Classica, GB–London
p. 127 (centre)	James Newton, GB–London
p. 127 (right)	Antje Stamm, D–Bermersheim / Winfried Klein, D–Budenheim
p. 128	Linda Blatzek, D–Trier
p. 129 (left)	Tom Gundelwein, D–Saarbrücken
p. 129 (centre)	Rainer Hoheisel, D–Guelder
p. 129 (right)	Uwe Dettmar, D–Frankfurt am Main
p. 130 (right)	Susanne Sommerfeld, D–Constance
p. 130 (centre)	Sabine Hauf, D–Berlin
p. 130 (left)	Peter Quirin, D–Wiesbaden
p. 131	BECKER'S Genuss AG, D–Trier
pp. 132, 133 (centre)	Zooey Braun, D–Stuttgart
p. 133 (left)	Otto Kasper, D–Rielasingen-Worblingen
p. 133 (right)	Michael Conrad, D–Bernkastel-Kues
p. 134 (left)	Markus Weiß, D–Seevetal
p. 134 (centre)	Heiko Gruber, D–Rüdesheim an der Nahe
p. 134 (right)	Egon Wurm/DPA/Adagp
p. 135	Mark Sengstbratl, A–Linz
p. 136 (left)	Ulrich Egger, I–Merano
p. 136 (centre)	Eugeni Pons, E–Lloret
p. 136 (right)	OHLA Hotel, E–Barcelona
p. 137 (left)	Javier Aisa, E–Madrid
p. 137 (centre)	Fernando Alda, E–Seville
p. 137 (right)	Carlos Glera, E–Logroño
p. 138	Eugeni Pons, E–Lloret
p. 139 (left)	Melanie Brunner Lutze, CH–Berneck
p. 139 (centre)	Anders Westerholm, FIN–Helsinki
p. 139 (right)	Bertalan Soós, H–Budapest

Section header images
p. 8/9	Susanne Sommerfeld, D–Constance
p. 24/25	Francesco Galli, I–Viterbo
p. 124/125	Andreas Burghardt, A–Vienna

Partner

DETAIL would like to thank the following sponsor for their support of this publication:

n&co Floors GmbH & Co.KG, Düsseldorf

Authors

Heinz-Gert Woschek
born in 1937
Born in one of the best vintage years, Heinz-Gert Woschek was lucky enough to be exposed to the world of wine at a very early point in his career. He has dedicated most of his life to the world of wine culture.

Woschek has worked in public relations for national agricultural and wine institutions in Germany, France, Italy and Austria. As an author, he has written a number of texts and handbooks on wine, gastronomy and tourism. He has also produced various television and radio programmes and held trade fairs, seminars and workshops.
In addition to acting as publisher and editor of wine and travel magazines (such as *Alles über Wein*, *reisen & genießen*), he has set up and moderated symposia on wine and architecture in collaboration with the Rhineland-Palatinate Chamber of Architects.

Denis Duhme
born in 1966
Having studied forestry and economics at Freiburg, Denis Duhme worked in engineered wood products manufacturing in a managerial capacity and was a partner and managing director of a parquet flooring manufacturer. Since 2012, he has been a managing partner of n&co Floors, Düsseldorf.

Apart from hunting, Duhme's great passion is wine. In order to acquire an in-depth knowledge in the field, he spent several years training to become a wine expert at the Austrian Wine Academy in collaboration with the Wine & Spirit Education Trust (WSET) in London. Thereafter he founded the "wein-intensiv" wine school in Cologne. Duhme is the author of *weinkompakt*, a small wine handbook targeted at wine novices as well as connoisseurs. At his own vineyard near the Ruwer river, he has been producing Riesling varieties for the past six years.

Katrin Friederichs
born in 1971
After studying German and English studies, education and philosophy in Duisburg, Katrin Friederichs has been marketing manager of Zeter – Die Weinagentur GmbH & Co KG, a wholesale distributor of wine in Neustadt/Weinstraße, since 2011.

Ever since university, the multi-faceted wine expert has been passionately interested in the world of wine. In addition to her many years of experience in the wine industry, primarily in sales and marketing, Friederichs has a long and successful track record in hosting seminars and further development courses.
A native of the Ruwer valley, during her time in Germany's Mosel and Pfalz regions she began to write about the "most fascinating drink in the world", and the people and landscapes that bring it to life.